D0368205

THE ENJOYMENT
of
CHESS PROBLEMS

BY KENNETH S. HOWARD

with 200 Illustrative Positions by the Author

Fourth Edition

DOVER PUBLICATIONS, INC.
NEW YORK

Published in Canada by General Publishing Company, Ltd., 30 Lesmill Road, Don Mills, Toronto, Ontario.

Published in the United Kingdom by Constable and Company, Ltd., 10 Orange Street, London WC 2.

This Dover edition, first published in 1961, is an unabridged and revised republication of the second edition as published by Bell Publishing Company in 1951.

Fourth revised edition published by Dover Publications, Inc., in 1967.

Standard Book Number: 486-20742-0
Library of Congress Catalog Card Number: 61-1979

Manufactured in the United States of America
Dover Publications, Inc.
180 Varick Street
New York, N.Y. 10014

Note to the Fourth Edition

SINCE the publication of the earlier editions of THE ENJOYMENT OF CHESS PROBLEMS a number of the problemists mentioned in the text have died, including Alain White, Godfrey Heathcote, A. J. Fink and C. S. Kipping, and the years of their deaths are given in this edition. There are also a number of textual alterations.

K. S. H.

Dover, New Jersey
April, 1967

Note to the Second Edition

THE publication of this second edition of THE ENJOY-MENT OF CHESS PROBLEMS affords a welcome opportunity to correct some inaccuracies in the text of the first edition, to substitute new problems for two that were discovered to be unsound, and to replace several other problems with positions the author considers of greater interest.

When the first edition was published, Wilhelm Wendell, of Phoenix, Arizona, solved all of the problems without referring to the printed solutions. In doing so, he found a cook, that could not be remedied, to the four-mover given as No. 105, for which another problem is substituted in this edition. Godfrey Heathcote called attention to a thematic dual in No. 145, but fortunately it was easy to correct.

The author is grateful to these friends for examining the positions so carefully. He also is indebted to Dr. M. Niemeijer, C. S. Kipping and Eric M. Hassberg for furnishing data regarding various European composers, and to A. J. Fink for testing the new positions included in this edition.

Preface

THERE are thousands of chess players who pay little or no attention to problems, or who are merely desultory solvers, and it is the author's belief that a large percentage of these would take a real interest in problems, and get a keen pleasure from solving, if they understood the fundamentals of problem composition. Accordingly it is to aid any chess lover to get greater enjoyment from problems that the author has written this book.

To this end the arrangement and treatment of the material has been made popular rather than technical. A knowledge of the moves of the chessmen is presupposed, but no further chess experience is demanded of the reader, although it naturally is hoped that many persons, who already have a more or less wide acquaintance with problems, will find the volume of value. The illustrative problems are selected from the thousand odd that the author has composed over a period sufficiently long to have seen many changes in the ideals of composition.

It seemed desirable to explain at the beginning of the book some of the more common terms of the problemist's vocabulary, and this is done in the introductory chapter. The majority of the technical terms, however, are defined when the occasion first arises to use them in discussions of various subjects throughout the book. When the name of a composer is first mentioned it is followed by the year of his birth or, if he is no longer living, by the years of his birth and death. This is so that any reader, who may not be familiar with the composer's work, will know whether the composer is of the present or of a past generation.

Some readers who prefer to solve problems for themselves instead of having the solutions shown to them, may wish to solve the illustrative problems before reading the text. For this reason the solutions are not printed with the problems but are given at the end of the chapters. The name of the magazine or newspaper given above a problem is that in which the problem was first published, and the date of publication is given in each instance. A "V" (version) before the name of the periodical indicates that since its first publication the problem has been revised, either because it was found to be unsound or to have some serious flaw.

The modified algebraic notation used throughout the book in giving the solutions is the form that the author employs in the *American Chess Bulletin's* problem section, which he has edited for the past eight years. Those who are not familiar with this notation will find it explained at the end of Chapter One. For the last seventeen years, the author, for the sake of uniformity, has diagrammed his problems with the white king on his own side of the board. The only exception to this practice is in the case of certain castling problems, in which the white king is required on the queen's side.

All the illustrative problems in this book have been published previously in chess magazines or in the chess columns of newspapers, and presumably were tested by the solvers of such magazines and columns more or less carefully. In the case of several such publications, however, which did not have strong corps of solvers, the author has been skeptical of how thoroughly the problems may have been tested. Accordingly he asked two skillful solvers, Carl Weberg, of Salina, Kansas, and Harry Conover, of Elberon, New Jersey, to examine positions about whose soundness he had any doubt. Mr. Weberg and Mr. Conover have solved over eighty of the two hundred problems in the book, testing them both for possible cooks and for the presence of thematic or major duals. Mr. Weberg found four of the author's favorite four-movers to be faulty and also cooked some of the three-movers. Mr. Conover carefully checked the corrected versions of a number of positions that had proved to be unsound on first publication. The author is grateful to both of these friends for their painstaking analyses and cooperation.

The manuscript of the book was read by Alain White, who made many constructive criticisms and important suggestions, all of which have been incorporated in the final version, and the author is deeply appreciative of Mr. White's valuable and enthusiastic aid. The author's indebtedness to Mr. White, however, goes far deeper than for his assistance in connection with this present volume.

The author's composing experience is divided into two periods, since he did no composing between 1908 and 1923. In the earlier period of his work, during which his compositions were restricted to two-movers, he had corresponded frequently with Mr. White in regard to themes. When he again took up composition in 1923, he started with three-movers of Bohemian type, and resumed his correspondence with Mr. White, whose suggestions and encouragement at that time were a great incentive. In addition to Mr. White's help through personal correspondence, the author owes a large debt to Mr. White's *Christmas Series,* which those who are familiar with the volumes of that series will realize as they read this book. Many volumes of the *Christmas Series* directly influenced the author in the composition of various large groups of problems; notably such volumes as *Bohemian Garnets, The White Rooks* and *More White Rooks, Running the Gauntlet, The Theory of Pawn Promotion, Changing Fashions,* and *The Properties of Castling.* In fact, the reader will note that in this book separate chapters are devoted to Pawn Promotion Themes, En Passant Pawn Captures, Castling Themes, and the White Rooks, the problems illustrating each of these chapters having been composed as the direct result of studies of the corresponding books in the *Christmas Series.*

KENNETH S. HOWARD

East Orange, New Jersey
June, 1943

Contents

THE ENJOYMENT OF
CHESS PROBLEMS

Introductory

THERE is an essential distinction between a chess problem and a composed endgame. In an endgame the solver has to demonstrate a win or draw for white against a superior, or at least an equal, force, and is allowed an indefinite number of moves in which to do so. The point of the endgame is based on the difference in the apparent relative material strength of white and black. In a problem it is not a question of relative strength but of the possibility of showing a mate against any defense in a limited number of moves. In an endgame the solver is fighting against *material* odds; in a problem he is fighting against *time*.

The modern chess problem is an illustration of some particular powers of the chess men in their interaction with one another. The chess problem is not primarily merely a puzzle. Even the term itself is a misnomer if it is used in a limited sense, since difficulty of solution is only one of the many desirable elements in a chess problem.

In *Mate in Two Moves*, Brian Harley *(1883–1955)* describes a chess problem as "a position constructed to display, to best advantage, an idea (or combination of ideas) that leads to forced mate in a definite number of moves.

The composer of a problem may wish to illustrate a series of ingenious attacking or defending manoeuvres, or he may concentrate on other points, such as pure deception of the solver, a peculiar set of mating positions, repetition of a particular strategic device, or just a whimsical fancy of his own."

Although the composition of chess problems dates back over a thousand years into the Middle Ages, the foundations of the problem of today were laid a century ago by the composers of what are now called The Old School. The problems of these composers were to a large extent based on forced sacrifices and checking continuations running into many moves, with little or no choice of defensive play. Gamelike positions were regarded as so desirable a feature that men frequently were added, which took no part in the play, merely to give the appearance of relatively equal forces. This period was followed by that of The Transition School, on which H. G. M. Weenink (*1892–1931*) comments in *The Chess Problem*: "The period between 1845 and 1862 is of the utmost importance in the history of the development of the chess problem. It was the trial period of the young art, during which the principal themes found their first clear cut presentation. The old masters . . . showed how the problem technique, the outward form and method for the expression of chess thoughts, could be refined and improved. During the Transition Period, the ideas which deserved expression were discovered. There was no systematic search for new ideas; their very profusion enabled the composer to pick up his themes almost at random; so that, as the number of composers increased, even this unsystematic kind of investigation brought to light the fundamentals of a great majority of our modern themes."

Once a definite study of specific themes began to be

undertaken it gradually came to be recognized that aesthetically it was desirable to illustrate them without unnecessary moves. For example, it was realized that it was inartistic to take six or seven moves to show a theme which required only three for its presentation. Present-day problems are nearly all two-movers and three-movers; four-movers or longer problems are now composed only where the character of the theme requires that length for its development.

In modern composition the distinction between two-movers and longer problems has come to be far more than a mere difference in lengths of solution; modern two-movers being essentially different in their nature from longer problems. The two-mover is not of sufficient length for the development of any deep strategic combinations, but though limited in this respect it has compensating advantages, in that it is possible to show much more variety in the defense than usually is practicable in a longer problem. It is common in a two-mover for black to have six or seven major defensive moves, each leading to a different and interesting mate by white. Although there is no theoretical limit to the number of major variations in a three-mover or four-mover, the difficulties of practical composition ordinarily limit the composer to three or four major lines.

Nowadays the increasing attention given to complex themes tends to reduce the number of variations both in two-movers and longer problems. Variety in itself is not now considered essentially desirable, unless it is related to the thematic content of the problem. The two-move form, however, permits a much greater degree of complexity in the individual variation than usually can be attained in longer problems, and the practical distinction between the average modern two-mover and longer problem is very marked. Accordingly in this volume two-movers are treated by themselves.

In the remaining pages of this chapter the conventions that apply to problem composition are described, and some of the problemistic terms in common use are defined. Other terms, as they occur, will be explained in later chapters.

Problems that employ the same men and type of board used by players, and in which white mates black in a specified number of moves, are termed *orthodox problems,* and are the only kind that come within the scope of this volume, with the exception of self-mates. Many composers are experimenting with men of different powers and boards of different types from those used in the game. Problems with such features, and also those in which the play is subject to special conditions, are termed *Fairy problems,* and this branch of composition is called *Fairy Chess.* Since this book is designed primarily for the chess player, who perhaps may have only a slight acquaintance with problems, the author has thought best to restrict its contents to the forms of composition most closely associated with the game. The final chapter treats of self-mates, but when these are of the usual form they may be considered orthodox as compared with the various types of modern Fairy compositions.

Actually there are only a few conventions that have to be observed in the composing of chess problems. As a matter of convenience white always is assumed to move first in orthodox problems and to mate black, except in the case of self-mates where white forces black to deliver the mate. The one convention that is invariably enforced is that a problem must be a position possible to reach in a game, however improbable or artificial the arrangement of the men may appear.

Only pieces that would be on the board at the beginning of a game are permitted in the initial position of a problem. For example, it is not permissible to have three white knights or two white king's bishops. In the solution of a problem, however, pawns may be promoted to pieces irrespective of what are already on the board, as in the playing of the game.

Sometimes a piece is found in the initial position of a problem that must have resulted from a pawn promotion. For example, if a white king's bishop is present, not on its home square, and if white's king's and king's knight's pawns are on their home squares, it is proof that the bishop must have come from a pawn promotion. Such a man is termed an *obtrusive piece* and its use is deprecated. In fact some critics regard a problem with such a piece inadmissible as a tourney entry.

Of the special chess moves, pawn promotions always are permissible, either as keys or during the after-play. En passant pawn captures are allowed if they take place as legitimate moves during the course of the solution, but they may be used as keys only if a *retrograde analysis* of the position proves that black's last move must have been the advance of a pawn two squares, making the en passant capture a legal move.

Whether either white or black has the right to castle can never be proved, unless one has the complete score of a game leading to the problem position. Consequently various authorities have objected to any use of castling in problems. On the other hand many interesting strategic effects can be obtained through castling, and, in recent years especially, numerous "castling problems" have been composed. These are discussed in detail in Chapter Fifteen.

The first move in a problem is termed the *key*. Ordinarily it should be an apparently aimless move; one which on the surface does not seem strong from a playing point of view. There is no rule against the employment of any legitimate move as a key, but in common practice all obviously strong or aggressive moves are avoided. This includes not only checking moves and captures, but also moves which reduce the freedom of the black king or decrease the possible activity of any of the other black men, either by pinning or other means. A move which brings a white man toward the black king, or into a more seemingly attacking position is undesirable. The promotion of a pawn to a piece usually is objectionable because it palpably increases the power of the white forces. It is also undesirable to move a white man from a square where it is attacked to one where it is out of danger.

Conversely, moves are theoretically good as keys that give more freedom to the black king or other black men, or that seem to reduce the attacking power of white. Thus a move that withdraws a white man from the vicinity of the black king to a square where its power seems less dangerous is a desirable key.

In recent years the capturing of a black pawn as a key is looked upon with more leniency than formerly, particularly when the captured pawn has no defensive value, or when the capture self-pins the white man that makes it, so that the move actually seems to reduce or even nullify the capturing man's attacking power.

In three- and four-move, or longer, problems, it naturally is desirable if white's ensuing moves, prior to the mating moves, instead of being checks or captures, can also have some of the qualities just described as being desirable in keys. Where the white moves prior to the mating moves are not checks or captures, they are spoken of as *quiet moves*.

There must be only one first move that will solve a problem; otherwise the problem is termed *unsound* and is valueless. When other first moves, besides the one intended by the composer as the key, are found to solve a problem, they are said to be *cooks,* and a problem proved to be unsound in this way is *cooked.*

A problem also is unsound when it is found to have no solution; some unexpected defense of black defeating the composer's intended key. A third type of unsoundness is where the initial position of the problem is one that would be impossible to reach in actual play.

In the ideal problem, after any move of black, white should have only one move that will lead to mate in the required number of moves, but this is not always possible in practical composition. In two-move problems, where white after a black move has a choice of two mating moves, they are termed dual mates, or more briefly, *duals.* Where there are three such possible moves they are sometimes called *triples,* and more than three are *multiples.* The word duals, however, frequently is used in a generic sense to cover all cases where white has a choice of more than one mating move. In three-movers and longer problems, when white has a choice of procedure on the second move, or on any other move prior to the mating move, it is called a *dual continuation* and ordinarily is a more serious defect than is a dual mate. Dual continuations are often merely termed duals.

There is considerable variation in the character and objectionableness of duals. A dual or dual continuation may parallel a mate or continuation that illustrates the theme of the problem, and which is accordingly termed *thematic.* This makes it possible for white to mate in that line of play without necessarily making the thematic moves, and so such a dual or dual continuation is called a *thematic dual.* It is the most obnoxious kind and ruins the value of the problem. It ranks next to actual unsoundness as a compositional defect.

Duals also are classified as major and minor. In a *major dual* white has a choice of lines of play and there is one of them which he is not forced to adopt by any of black's defenses. In a *minor dual* white has a choice following indifferent defensive moves, but black can make certain moves which compel white to adopt in turn each of the possible continuations. Duals occurring in unthematic or in secondary lines of play are also sometimes called minor duals. They are considered of the least importance and they are even disregarded by many composers. In the past the English composers as a whole have been most insistent on exact accuracy in composition. Composers of other countries have preferred to sacrifice some accuracy rather than to employ additional force to ensure it in unthematic continuations. By permitting duals in unthematic lines it often is possible to secure greater depth or more sparkle in the thematic play. Accordingly the question of whether to tolerate minor duals is a matter of individual taste on the part of the composer, although every composer naturally prefers to have his work as accurate as possible, if it does not involve any sacrifice of other desirable qualities.

In the construction of chess problems the terms applied to certain important features may require elucidation for the reader to understand the sense in which they are used. Thus for example, economy in the composition of a problem does not necessarily mean the employment of few men. *Economy* refers to the relation between the number of men used and the results obtained, usually measured by the variety or the complexity of the lines of play. A problem is said to be constructed uneconomically when the same results could have been secured either with fewer men or with less powerful ones.

It is desirable to have the men employed perform as many functions as possible, and the more important the pieces the greater should be their duties. A black pawn may be used solely to block a square in a single line of play without any breach of economy, but if the white queen is on the board it is desirable, whenever possible, to have her take part in every thematic line, although in the case of some types of two-movers this is not practicable. In three-movers and longer problems there is more opportunity than in two-movers for a composer to show his skill in handling the forces economically. For instance, in a three-mover, a white piece may make the second move in one continuation, make the mating move in a second continuation, and act as a guarding piece in other lines of play.

A problem involving the use of a large number of men may actually be more economically constructed than some lightweight, if the heavier position shows a proportionately greater amount of play for the men employed than does the lighter one. Finally, as a rule, economy in the functioning of the white forces is regarded as of greater importance than in the case of the black forces.

Difficulty of solution is always a relative quality, since a problem that may prove extremely difficult for one solver, may be solved easily by another. The experienced solver frequently perceives at once the theme that the composer is illustrating and this may lead quickly to the discovery of the key and the principal continuations. The inexperienced solver may follow some hit-and-miss method of solving and he may base his opinion of the difficulty of the problem on the length of time he happens to require to find the solution.

Sometimes a poorly constructed problem by a beginner in composition may puzzle an experienced solver simply because the theme is crudely presented and not clean-cut, as in the work of an adept composer. Furthermore, in such a problem the veteran solver may be searching for beauties that the position does not contain and actually overlook the solution because it is so obvious, while the tyro in solving might chance on the key immediately. Then mere complexity should not be confused with difficulty. Many complicated positions oblige the solver to take considerable time to perceive the purposes and relations of the men, but as soon as he has done this the solution becomes apparent. This frequently is the case with complex two-movers.

One of the most desirable types of difficulty arises when the setting disguises even from experienced solvers the theme of the problem. Sometimes the initial position is definitely arranged to present a deceptive appearance, so as to inveigle the solver to look for a different theme from the one actually shown. Another feature that increases difficulty of solution is the presence of one or more plausible lines of attack which are defeated only by obscure defenses.

A specious first move is termed a *try*, and the construction of a problem is particularly meritorious where there is but a single defense of black that frustrates the try. If a try leads to thematic play it is even more likely to deceive the experienced solver, since it tends strongly to make him believe he is on the right track. Such a try occurs in problem 80 in Chapter Eight, the move 1 Qg6 leading to two thematic lines of play, related to but differing from those in the true solution.

In most instances the composer does not work primarily

for these effects because the proper illustration of the theme is his first consideration. If in addition to this, however, he is able to introduce one or more plausible tries or to secure a deceptive setting, it enhances the interest of the composition and increases the solver's pleasure when he finally succeeds in unraveling the solution.

The general appearance of a problem either may attract or repel a solver, and most composers endeavor to secure as attractive settings as possible for their compositions. A century ago it was regarded as desirable to have problems present a gamelike appearance and to produce this effect men often were added which took no part in the actual solution. This practice was termed "dressing the board." It is indeed a far cry from such a custom to the present emphasis on economy of material.

Of course the arrangement of men in the average problem is highly artificial from the viewpoint of a player, but the skilled composer endeavors to keep his positions from appearing too unnatural. It is preferable to have the men, as far as possible, spaced over the entire board rather than to be congested in one section of it. Especially is it desirable to have at least some of the squares around the black king unoccupied. Six or seven men on adjacent squares present an unpleasantly crowded effect. Most composers try to avoid using any great number of pawns, particularly white ones. Pairs of mutually blocking white and black pawns produce an unpleasant effect, and doubled or tripled pawns are objectionable, except when they are used thematically. Even the placing of pieces in unnatural, although legal, positions is avoided whenever practicable by good composers.

When a problem has but few pawns, has the pieces evenly scattered over the board, and has several vacant squares around the black king, it is called an *open* or a *natural* position, and unquestionably it is the type that is most likely to tempt a solver to try his skill.

Besides endeavoring to avoid objectionable constructive features in the initial setting of a problem, the good composer also tries to avoid objectionable features in the solution. One of the most common of these is a too aggressive threat, which often is termed "brutal." An example is a threatened mate in a two-mover involving the capture of a major piece without any compensating effects. Another example is a second-move threat in a three-mover which combines a capture and a check. In a three-mover or longer problem, a threatened mate in less than the stipulated number of moves is called a *short mate* and is regarded as a demerit.

By a polished composition is meant a problem that combines the good qualities described in the preceding pages; attractiveness of setting, economy of presentation and sufficient difficulty or unexpectedness in the character of the solution to make the solver feel that he is well repaid for his efforts.

Because, in the modern problem, mate usually has to be given in two, three, or four moves, the majority of the lines of force of the white pieces must, in most instances, converge toward the black king. Black's lines of defense also must as a rule center around the black king. This is not necessarily the case in an endgame, where the decision often may be forced on a part of the board far from the black king's station.

When a long-range white piece—queen, rook, or bishop—is on a line with the black king and only a single black man intervenes, the latter will be *pinned,* a term familiar to the player. When a man is released from a pin it is *unpinned.* When either white or black moves so as to pin

one of his own men the action is termed *self-pinning.*
Half-pinning will be described in Chapter Six. Pinning
and unpinning play an exceedingly important role in
modern chess problems.

If instead of having a black man intervening, there is a
white one on the line between a long-range white piece
and the black king, the two white men are said to form
a *battery.* A movement of the intervening white man off
the line will discover check, which is spoken of as *firing*
the battery. Besides being aimed at the black king, batteries also may be aimed at a square adjacent to the one
on which the king stands. The former type of battery is
termed a *direct,* the latter an *indirect* one. The firing of an
indirect battery may open a line of guard on a hitherto
unguarded square next to the black king and at the same
time the firing piece itself may check the king. This occurs
not infrequently in two-movers. Batteries commonly are
designated according to the type of the front or firing
man, as for example, a knight battery or a pawn battery.

If in addition to the white intervening piece there also
is a black one on the line between the white attacking
piece and the black king, the arrangement is a *mixed* or
masked battery. In such a case the black king can not be
checked unless the black man first moves off the line. On
the other hand, if the white firing piece moves first it
will leave the black man pinned. Various forms of batteries, in combination with pinning and unpinning maneuvers, make up a great part of the mechanism of a large
percentage of problems.

When the rear piece of a battery is not already in position but moves there in the course of the solution of a
problem, it is said to form an *ambush.* In fact this term is
applied whenever a long-range piece moves onto a line
with the opposing king on which there are intervening

men, if the move is made with the purpose of later discovering check or guarding a piece next to the king, or to effect a pin when some man withdraws from the line.

Decoy is a term that is much used in a technical sense in problem terminology. When by a white maneuver a black man is drawn away from guarding a square, or is drawn off a line that it is obstructing, it is said to be decoyed. Examples of decoys will be found in many of the illustrative problems; particularly in a number of the compositions given in Chapter Twelve.

The notation used in this book is the *algebraic,* or a modified form of what is sometimes called the *Continental,* because the latter is used in many European countries. It is both more concise and more precise than the English notation. From the white side of the board, or

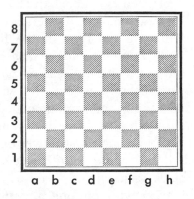

the bottom of a diagram, the files from left to right are lettered a to h. The ranks are numbered 1 to 8 from the white side of the board, or from the lower rank of a diagram. Accordingly white's queen's rook's square is designated a1 and black's king's rook's square h8.

The same letters for the men are used as in the English notation, except that S (German *Springer*) designates the knight. 0 – 0 is Castles KR: 0 – 0 – 0 is Castles QR. The symbol x is used for capture.

As an illustration, the moves written in English notation as 1 P – K4, P – K4; 2KKt – B3, P – Q3; 3 P – Q4, KKt – B3; 4 Kt – B3, QKt – Q2; would be written in the notation used in this book, 1 Pe4, Pe5; 2 Sf3, Pd6; 3 Pd4, Sf6; 4 Sc3, Sb8 – d7.

Types of Two-Movers

FROM a constructional point of view it is customary to divide two-move problems into two great groups, depending on whether, after the keymove is made, a mate is threatened on the next move. When a definite mate is threatened by white the problem is known as a *threat problem*. Various moves by black that prevent the threatened mate allow white to mate in other ways. Such defenses with the ensuing mates are termed *variations*.

For example, in problem 1 the keymove is 1 Sd1, threatening 2 Sc3 mate. Black has four different ways to defeat this threat. He can do it by capturing the white rook with his king, queen or bishop, or by capturing the king's pawn with the rook, which removes the guard of the queen's pawn. While these moves defeat the threat, they permit white to mate in new ways, which make the variations of the problem. Three of these captures result in black self-blocks, a term which will be explained in Chapter Four.

When a two-mover is composed to illustrate some sharply defined theme, in many cases the composer finds it easiest, from a constructional point of view, to have the keymove introduce a threatened mate that may not necessarily be related to the theme, and then to bring in the thematic play as defenses to that threat.

The second great group of two-movers includes the various forms of *waiting move* problems. In these the keymove does not set up any mating threat, and if black did not have to play white could not mate on the second move. Black being forced to move, however, is obliged to weaken one or another of his defenses or to move his king into a mating position, thus enabling white to deliver the respective mates that the composer has prepared.

Waiting move problems are subdivided into *incomplete* and *complete block* positions. In the former mates are set for several of black's defenses, but not for every one of them. Accordingly it is necessary for the keymove to provide mates for whatever black moves do not have set mates awaiting them. Occasionally an incomplete block problem has no mates whatsoever set in the initial position and the keymove, although not threatening mate, makes possible all the mates that actually occur after black is forced to move.

In the complete block position, on the other hand, there is a mate set for every move black can make, and black would be mated if he moved first. So black is said to be "blocked." In this type of position the keymove either has to be one that does not disturb the mating arrangements or one that provides new mates to take the place of any set mates that may be affected. In the former case white simply has to "lose a move," and these problems are relatively easy to solve by the merely mechanical process of determining which white move will not disarrange the set mates. In the latter case the keymove changes the arrangement so that one or more of the set mates are abandoned and new mating positions take their place. Such problems are more difficult to solve and much more interesting than are those in which the key merely gains a tempo. Twenty years ago complete blocks, with changed or added mates, were much the vogue; special tourneys were held limited to this form of two-mover, and one leading English chess column published no other kind of two-move problems.

Problem 2 is an example of an incomplete block position. If black should move first there are mates provided for 1 — — Kd4 and 1 — — Kf6, but not for 1 — — KxQP and 1 — — Kf4. The keymove makes provision for mates for these moves, without changing the other two mates already set. Problem 8 is another incomplete block. An examination of the position will show that mates are prepared for every move of black except 1 — — Kc3. After this move there would be a mate by 2 Se2 if the pawn at c2 were guarded. This can be done by 1 Rc1, but this move removes the guard from e5, yielding the black king a second flight square. If black plays 1 — — Ke5, however, there is a mate by 2 Sf3. Thus the position is an incomplete block problem with an *added mate*.

Since to solve a pure waiting move problem it is merely necessary to find a move that does not alter the existing mating arrangements in any way, even a solver of limited experience can readily discover the key by the routine process of examining in turn each possible black move, noting the mate provided for it, and then by elimination determining what particular white move will not affect any mating provisions. Problem 15, in the next chapter, is of this type and the task for the solver is merely to find a move for white that does not alter the set mating positions.

Pure waiting move problems seldom appear nowadays since the modern composer in planning a complete block composition usually prefers to construct one in which the key either adds new mates or changes some of the mates set in the initial position. Frequently the composer succeeds in doing both. Where new mates are added the com-

1

*Entry in 13th International
Tourney
The Sydney Morning Herald
1908*

White mates in two moves

2

*The Literary Digest
July 30, 1904*

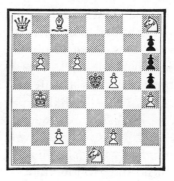

White mates in two moves

3

*American Chess Bulletin
July–August, 1938*

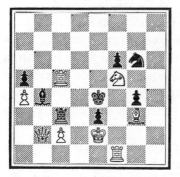

White mates in two moves

4

*Commended, First Tourney
of National Chess Federation
of U. S. A., 1928*

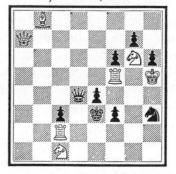

White mates in two moves

position is known as an added-mate waiter; where mates are changed the problem is termed a changed-mate waiter, or a *mutate*, a happily descriptive name coined by Brian Harley, chess editor of the London *Observer* and author of *Mate in Two Moves* and of other works on chess subjects.

For an illustration of the mutate examine problem 3. In the initial position there are mates set for any move black may make. Note the possible moves of the black rook, particularly 1 — — Rc4 and 1 — — RxR. After the former there is a mate by 2 Sd6 and after the latter by 2 Qd4. If 1 — — RxP ck; 2 QxR. If 1 — — Rd3; 2 PxR. If 1 — — Ra3 or b3, there are dual mates, either 2 Sd6 or 2 Qd4. Now if a pure waiting move for white could be found, so as to gain a tempo, the problem would be solved, but no such waiting move is possible. The keymove turns out to be 1 Qb1. The mate following 1 — — Rc4 is changed to 2 Pc3; that after 1 — — RxR to 2 Pc4. The dual disappears, since after 1 — — Ra3 white must play 2 Pc3, and after 1 — — Rb3; 2 PxR, an added line of play. The mates following the moves of the black bishop and the black knight are not changed by the keymove.

In problem 79 there are five set mates in the initial position, while in the actual play two of the original black moves no longer are possible and two new lines take their place. This latter mutate was composed not merely for the changed mates but primarily to illustrate a complex theme, to which the mutate setting is a secondary consideration.

Another type of changed-mate problem is called the *block-threat*, because it has the initial setting of a complete block position but is solved by a threat key. Actually such compositions are threat problems, but constructionally they are more closely related to complete blocks.

No. 4 is an illustration of this type. In the initial position a mate is provided for every possible black move, but white can not make any tempo gaining move. The key is 1 Rc5, threatening 2 Rc5xP. This keymove changes all but two of the initial mating positions, and also, by unpinning the black queen, introduces new mates after 1 — — Qc4, 1 — — Qd5 ck and 1 — — Qe5 ck. Problem 16 is also a block-threat.

Interesting effects sometimes are obtained by a change of mates in one or two of the more prominent lines of play in a threat problem. In fact, problems of this type often are the most difficult to solve of any kind of two-movers, because the solver sees from the general construction that they are not block problems and hence he is not expecting to find changes in prominent mates that are already set. Of such a type is problem 14 in Chapter Three and problem 22 in Chapter Four.

In recent years by far the greater proportion of two-move compositions that have been published are threat rather than block positions. The use of a threat, as previously mentioned, is usually the more convenient constructional way of handling most types of themes, and the modern composer is emphatically interested in definite themes. Furthermore, during the last decade especial attention has been given to a study of two types of play specifically based on the threat form of two-mover.

The first of these types is termed *dual avoidance*. In *A Century of Two-Movers*, Alain White *(1880–1951)* defines dual avoidance: "The theme of dual avoidance implies the presence in a problem of two or more variations with Black defences of a similar kind, which in each case seem to allow two mates, also of similar kind, but one of them is avoided in an artistic manner. For the theme to stand out clearly, the method of suppressing the duals should be similar in both variations . . . the impending dual of one variation may be realized in the actual play of the second variation, and *vice versa.*"

This feature is illustrated in problem 5. The key is 1 Qa5, threatening 2 Qd5, and black's thematic defenses are 1 — — Rd6 and 1 — — Re5. Either of these moves unpin white's king's rook, allowing it to check at e3 or g4, and at first glance there might seem to be dual mates. Before black moves white doubly guards the squares d4 and f5, but when black plays 1 — — Rd6 it shuts off the guard of white's queen's rook on d4, and if white replied 2 Re3 ck, the rook would interfere with white's queen's bishop, cutting off the second guard on d4. So white can mate only by 2 Rg4.

If black, on the other hand, defends by 1 — — Re5, it shuts off the queen's guard on f5, and if white plays 2 Rg4 ck, the guard by white's king's bishop is also cut off, so that the black king can escape to f5. Accordingly in this variation white must mate by 2 Re3. Note the similarity in the mechanism of both these variations, which is an essential element in this theme.

The second type of threat problem to which especial attention is being devoted today is one that contains a contingent threat accompanied by black correction play. Mr. White, in the volume already mentioned, succinctly explains these terms as follows: "In a threat problem, if the removal of a Black piece away from its original square in itself defeats the threat, irrespective of where it may be moved to, yet at the same time permits a new threat to become effective against purposeless moves of the Black piece, such a secondary threat is called a *Contingent Threat* and any defensive moves of the Black piece which defeat this contingent threat, as well as the original threat, are called *Black Corrections.*"

No. 6 was composed specifically to illustrate such black correction play. The key is 1 Rc4, threatening mate by 2 Sf4. Any move of the black rook on e5 will defeat this threat by opening a line for the black bishop to guard f4. Should black, however, make merely a random or "general" move, which in this case would mean playing the rook to any square but e4, white mates by 2 Rd4, the contingent threat. Such a move by black is an example of what is termed *compensating play*. The moving of the rook opens a line for the black bishop to guard f4 (an advantage for black), but as a compensation it also opens a line for the white bishop to guard d4 (an advantage for white).

To guard also against the contingent threat of 2 Rd4, black "corrects" his play and, instead of making merely a random move with the rook, plays 1 — — Re4. In addition to opening the guard of the white bishop on d4, this move proves to be a black self-block on e4 (explained in Chapter Four), and white now mates by 2 Rc5.

The moves of the black knight lead to another contingent threat, with black corrections. Any move of the knight, by opening a line for black's king's rook to guard f4, defeats the initial threat. A "general" move, however, such as to e3, e7, g7, h6 or h4, permits the contingent threat, 2 Be4, to operate. Black "corrects" this by 1 — — Sd4, but this move is again a self-block and white mates by 2 Rc5. There is a second correcting move by the knight, 1 — — Sd6, which is followed by 2 RxR.

Both dual avoidance and contingent threats with correction play are shown in problem 7. The key is 1 Sc3, threatening 2 Se2 mate. Instead of attempting to defeat the threat by guarding the square e2, black has a more subtle defense in simply moving the bishop, vacating the square d5 so that the white knight must remain on c3 to guard d5. The bishop initially guards both c4 and e4 against mate by one or the other of the white rooks. If the bishop makes a random move along the a2–g8 diagonal (to a2, b3, f7 or g8) white mates by 2 Re4. Should the bishop play to c4, however, it might seem at first to allow mate by either rook, leading to a dual. Actually the only mate is 2 RxB, because the black bishop has shut off the guard of the white bishop on d3, and should white attempt to mate by 2 Re4 ck, the rook would cut off white's second guard on d3, allowing the black king to escape to that square. Should the bishop move along the h1–a8 diagonal the play is similar. To any random move, such as 1 — — Bh1, g2, f3, b7 or a8, white replies 2 Rc4, but if 1 — — Be4, white cannot mate by 2 Rc4 ck, but again must capture the bishop.

The moves of the rooks to c4 or e4 are contingent threats, and black can defend against the original threat of 2 Se2 and also against both of the contingent threats by making either of two correcting moves, 1 — — Bc6 or 1 — — Be6. These defenses, however, unpin the white queen, allowing her to deliver mate from g1 or e4 respectively.

Problems often are composed in which especial attention is given to the character of the final mating positions, but nowadays such problems are nearly always three- or four-movers, since the thematic complexity of the average modern two-mover precludes much emphasis being placed on the character of the mating positions in themselves. So, though at this point, some of the terms applying to mating positions will be explained, the subject will be treated more extensively in Chapters Nine, Ten and Eleven, which deal with three- and four-movers.

When in the mating position each square in the black *king's field,* i. e., the square on which he stands and the

5

The Observer
September 8, 1935

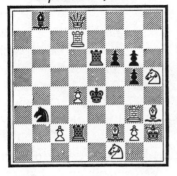

White mates in two moves

6

British Chess Magazine
January, 1941

White mates in two moves

7

V. L' Alfiere di Re
October–November, 1925

White mates in two moves

8

Norwich Mercury
October 5, 1904

White mates in two moves

ones immediately adjacent to it, either is guarded by a single white man or is occupied by a black one, the mate is termed *pure*. If, however, even a single square in the black king's field is guarded by two white men or is occupied by a black man and also guarded by a white one, the mate is *impure*. The only exception to this rule is where a black man that occupies a square next to the king is pinned by a white piece and could interpose to prevent the mate if it were not pinned. Examples of pure mates occur in problem 1 after 1 Sd1, threat 2 Sc3: 1 — — KxR; 2 Bc6: 1 — — BxR; 2 Se3: 1 — — QxR; 2 Qg8: and 1 — — RxP; 2 Rd4. In problems 2 and 8 all the mates are pure.

A generation ago much attention was paid to pure mates in two-movers and the reader will note that the three problems just referred to were composed during the first decade of the century. At that time the presence of one or more pure mates in a two-mover was regarded as a mark of constructive unity. With the intensive cultivation of complex two-move themes that was incited by The Good Companions, the presence of a pure mate in a two-mover has become a *rara avis*.

The Good Companion Chess Problem Club, popularly known as the "Good Companions," was an organization of problem composers founded in 1913 by J. F. Magee, Jr., (*1867-1955*) of Philadelphia. It became international in its membership, at one time including six hundred composers; finally disbanding after a decade of activity. The modern two-mover practically had its inception in the work of this club.

A pure mate where all the squares adjacent to the black king's are unoccupied and the king is not next to the edge of the board, is termed a *mirror mate*. Some authorities hold that to be a mirror mate it also must be a pure mate.

Although such a mate has some degree of attractiveness, possibly because it takes the mind a fraction of an instant longer than in the case of other mating positions to determine that the black king actually is mated, the mate in itself has no strategic interest. Since it is difficult to produce such mates in a problem of any thematic complexity, they seldom occur in modern composition and usually are found only in positions composed expressly to show such mates, as in problem 2. Here the black king has four diagonal *flight squares*, a term applied to unguarded and unoccupied squares adjacent to the one on which the black king stands, because he can flee to them. Such squares are sometimes briefly called *flights*. Positions like No. 2, in which the black king has four diagonal flights, have been named *star theme* problems. In No. 2 each move of the black king results in a mirror mate. When the black king can capture a white man, he is said to have a *flight capture*.

The British composer H. D'O. Bernard (*1878-1954*) is credited with the suggestion of the term *model mate* for one that is both pure and economical; a major feature in Bohemian-type compositions. The requisites for a pure mate have just been stated. An *economical mate* is one in which every one of the white men on the board takes some part, with the optional exception of the king and pawns. The solver, however, will seldom meet the term, since economical mates in themselves do not receive much attention from composers, being considered desirable only when they also are pure, thus constituting model mates. Because of the difficulty of combining them with the complex mechanism of the modern two-mover, model mates are now almost disregarded in the two-move field, but are of importance in certain types of problems in three and four moves. Model mates are shown in prob-

lem 1 in the variations 1 Sd1, KxR; 2 Bc6, and 1 — —
BxR; 2 Se3. There also are model mates in problem 13 in
the variations 1 PxP, Pc5; 2 QxB, and 1 — — Kd5; 2 QxB.

The term *task problem* is applied to compositions in
which the composer endeavors to show the maximum possibilities of the particular theme he is illustrating. In other
words he is attempting to make a record. Problem 2 comes
under this head, since the task the composer set himself
was to show mirror mates following each of the four diagonal flights of the black king.

In the latter part of the last century many efforts were
made to produce as many pure mates as possible in a two-
mover. For years the record had stood at six such mates,
but problem 8 shows nine technically distinct pure mates,
although the solver will see that several of these mates
are so similar that they have no individuality, and the
author doubts if it is possible to secure more than six entirely different pure mates in a two-mover. Such lines of
play in No. 8 as 1 — — Bg7 and 1 — — Bh8, followed by
2 QxB, count as distinct mates because the queen makes
the capture on different squares, but on account of their
similar nature they are called *concurrent mates,* and they
are only mildly interesting at the most. Likewise 1 — — S
any; 1 — — SPxP; and 1 — — BPxP, which are all followed by 2 Bb2, although technically distinct mates, have
too slight differences to be interesting.

In *Chess Lyrics,* the collection of problems by the great,
blind Jamaican composer, A. F. Mackenzie (*1861–1905*),
published in 1905 by Alain White, Mackenzie himself discussed pure mates at some length in the Introduction and
in several other places in the book, and problem 8 was
reproduced as position 265a in that volume. This is mentioned here merely as a matter of historical interest to
show how the aims of composers have changed in the last

forty years. Today the two-move composer is concerned chiefly with the illustration of complex strategic maneuvers and he would not think of attempting to produce a position merely to pile up the greatest possible number of pure mates.

SOLUTIONS

NO.1 1 Sd1	NO.4 1 Rc5	NO.7 1 Sc3
NO.2 1 Pf6	NO.5 1 Qa5	NO.8 1 Rc1
NO.3 1 Qb1	NO.6 1 Rc4	

The First Move

THE BEGINNER in problem solving usually is inclined to place an undue emphasis on the importance of white's first move, the *key* to the problem. A chess problem is not primarily a puzzle, and the keymove is only one of the many elements that make problems interesting. In order to solve a problem the keymove, of course, must be found, but in many problems, particularly in complex two-movers, the key frequently is of secondary importance.

It is not uncommon to have the idea that the composer is illustrating actually begin with black's defensive moves, and in such a case the key is essential only to make a conventionally sound problem. The experienced solver enjoys such a problem because of the manner in which a skillful composer expresses his idea. In the practical process of solving the problem, the solver probably will work out the variations first, beginning with black's moves, and come upon the correct key as an incident in the process. The author does not minimize the value of a fine keymove, but merely is explaining why the key often is subsidiary in importance to other elements of the problem.

In the ideal problem the keymove is an inherent part of the theme, or at least is closely related to it. Such a key is said to be *thematic*. Problems 3 and 4 necessarily have thematic keys, because in mutates and block-threats the keymoves change entirely the apparent character of the positions. In cross-check problems, described in the next chapter, a keymove is thematic which makes possible a check to the white king that cannot be given in the initial position.

In the practical composing of the majority of two-movers, the key is added after the construction of the problem otherwise is completed. There are cases, however, where the illustration of a striking keymove is in itself the chief idea of the problem and in such instances the position is built around the keymove, but of the two-movers composed today only a small percentage are of this type.

Whether a key is difficult to find ordinarily depends as much on the experience of the solver as on any other factor. A key which may be exceedingly hard for the tyro to discover, may be the first move that occurs to the solver who is familiar with problem themes. The type of key that appeals to the experienced solver is one that is thematic or spectacular or perhaps merely theoretically good. For example, long-range moves across the board or from corner to corner usually have a dramatic appeal, even though they may be comparatively easy to see. Keymoves that give the black king a flight square or which sacrifice a piece are theoretically good, yet they may be the first moves that a skilled solver will try.

Any apparently strong "playing" move makes a theoretically poor key. Poor keys of this character include moves that restrict not only the black king but any other black man. The essential objection to a capture as a keymove is that it obviously reduces black's defensive power. The pinning of a black man is nearly as objectionable, unless it can be regarded as thematic, as for example where black's defenses are designed to unpin such a man. Even in such a case there would be a question as to the expediency of its employment.

The movement of a white man toward the black king is likewise generally to be avoided in a keymove, as is the movement of any white man which seemingly is out of play in the initial position. There is no rule that the key cannot be a checking move, but since such a move is one of the most aggressive kind it is highly objectionable for a key, unless the check actually is part of the theme. Naturally every problem cannot have an ideal key and frequently the composer can do no better than to use one that is not definitely undesirable.

In *Mate in Two Moves*, Brian Harley grades the value of keys in order of increasing merit as follows:

1. Sacrificial
2. Flight giving
3. Self-pinning of a white man
4. Unpinning of a black man
5. Allowing a black check

A keymove may possess two or more of these characteristics, and if it does it is the more meritorious. The reader should carefully note the character of the keys of the illustrative problems in this book and evaluate them for himself. Some he will find good, some definitely thematic, some merely indifferent. Each of the eight problems given in this chapter was specifically built around its keymove. The keymove of problem 9 is of the striking type, designed to please the solver even if it does not prove to be difficult. That of problem 10 is perhaps somewhat more deceptive since it seemingly renders impotent the knight battery. Problem 11 was composed to prove delusive to the more experienced solver. The two succeeding problems, on the other hand, were composed to illustrate themes based primarily on the character of the keymoves. Whatever difficulty the solver may have in discovering them will be occasioned by the time it may take him to recognize the theme that the composer is illustrating.

The keymove of No. 9, 1 Bh6, is spectacular, taking the bishop from the vicinity of the black king to a distant edge of the board, where it is offered in sacrifice to a pawn, its capture permitting a long-range mate by the queen. This keymove also gives the black king a flight square, thus combining the first two characteristics in Harley's scale of key values. The key of No. 10 offers a flight capture, and it has in addition the unexpected feature of temporarily shutting off the white battery. The keymove actually leads to a threat of mate by the knight with the queen guarding the bishop, instead of having the knight give the discovered check that the initial setting suggests.

The next position was constructed with the specific intent of deceiving the more experienced solver rather than the beginner. Many problems have been composed showing a double en passant capture of a white pawn and veteran solvers are familiar with these problems and solve them automatically. Consequently when such a solver sees a position like No. 11 he naturally plays 1 Pc4, expecting the thematic play to arise from the en passant captures by the black pawns on b4 and d4. In this problems mates are provided for each of these captures, but nevertheless 1 Pc4 is merely a try, since black is given an adequate defense. White's threatened mate following 1 Pc4 is 2 Sd7 and there is only one black move that defends against this threat without permitting some other

mate. This move is 1 —— Rb5. The author intentionally
made this defense as obscure as he could. The actual key
is 1 Pc3, with the threat 2 QxKP.

The idea of No. 11 is not original with the author, but
it was suggested to him by a problem by the American
composer L. H. Jokisch (*1851–1938*), which was published originally in *Tidskrift for Schack* in 1909 and reproduced as No. 100 in Alain C. White's *Running the Gauntlet,* the only position in that volume in which the submit-
ting of a white pawn to the possibility of an en passant
capture figures as a try. The settings of the two problems,
however, are very different (Appendix A1).

In problem 12 the key, with the ensuing main-play,
constitutes the theme: 1 Rb6, RxP; 2 RxR. The name
American Indian was given to this theme by that great
American genius, Samuel Loyd (*1841–1911*), who illustrated it, although the English composer, B. G. Laws
(*1861–1931*), had shown the idea previously. This particular example was composed to show an "American Indian" in what is termed a "Meredith" setting. The Phila-
delphian composer William Meredith (*1835–1903*), particularly favored light-weight two-movers, and the Good
Companions honored his memory by applying the term
Meredith to two-movers which have a total of twelve or
less men.

A capture key is commonly considered objectionable
unless it is the capture of a black pawn by a white piece
that results in a self-pin of the latter. This occurs thematically in the Schór theme, an example of which is shown in
problem 78. A capture key also may be thematic when it
is used as in problem 13. Here the author's idea was to
produce a mate by means of two consecutive captures
made by a white pawn, and so the pawn captures in themselves form the theme of the problem. The key is 1 PxP,

9

Third Prize
Fourth Half-Yearly Tourney
Mid-week Sports Referee
February 17, 1927

White mates in two moves

10

The Observer
November 21, 1926

White mates in two moves

11

Cleveland vs. Cincinnati
Solving Contest
September, 1934
(The Cincinnati Enquirer
January 28, 1935)

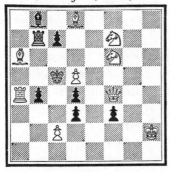

White mates in two moves

12

First Commended
Meredith Section
Falkirk Herald Tourney
1932–1933

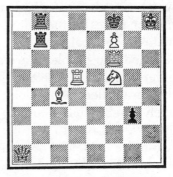

White mates in two moves

bringing the white pawn on the same file as the rook and forming a battery, with the threat of 2 PxP mate. This theme does not permit of much variety in secondary play and the author accordingly chose as light a setting as possible, so that the emphasis would be on the main-play.

Problem 14 has already been referred to in the preceding chapter as an example of changed mates in a threat problem. Any moves that can be made by the black king are always one of the first things in a problem to attract the attention of the experienced solver. In this problem it is at once seen that if 1 —— KxKP there is a mate by 2 Pd4. 1 —— PxS is also a prominent defensive move and 2 QPxP provides a pretty mate. Both of these apparent mating positions, however, are changed by the keymove, which is 1 Qg1. Now if 1 —— KxKP; 2 Pf4, and if 1 —— PxS; 2 Pf3. This latter line of play is an illustration of the Schiffmann defense, which is explained in Chapter Eight.

This particular problem has a further feature which is an unusual one. There is a try by 1 Qe1, threatening mate both by 2 QxP and 2 S any. Now if 1 —— KxKP; 2 QxP, black's queen's pawn being pinned. If 1 —— PxS; 2 Qe3. The author is not familiar with any other two-mover which has changed mates in a try, that differ both from the set mates in the initial position and from the actual mates in the real solution.

When two problems are similar except for some minor difference in their settings, but have different solutions, they are called *twins*. Commonly such positions are more likely to be found among longer problems than two-movers, but No. 15 and No. 16 illustrate twinning in the two-move field. The only difference in the settings is that the black knight on e8 in No. 15 is replaced with a black pawn on e7 in No. 16. This change, however, affects the

13

Grand Rapids Herald
March 19, 1933

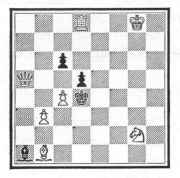

White mates in two moves

14

Third Honorable Mention
Informal Tourney
July–December, 1933
The Western Morning News
and Daily Gazette

White mates in two moves

15

American Chess Bulletin
July–August, 1925

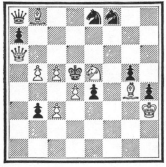

White mates in two moves

16

American Chess Bulletin
July–August, 1925

White mates in two moves

entire nature of the problems, for while No. 15 is a pure waiting move problem, No. 16 is a block-threat.

In the former white simply has to gain a tempo, which is done by playing 1 Bc7. This permits the black queen to reach c8, but if she moves there she no longer guards c6. In problem 16, on the other hand, if white tries 1 Bc7, black can reply 1 — — Qe8, retaining the guard on c6. The solution to this latter problem is 1 Qa1, threatening mate by 2 Pc4. This move will not solve No. 15 because then black can defend by 1 — — Sd6, but in No. 16 this knight is omitted.

SOLUTIONS

NO. 9	1 Bh6	NO.12	1 Rb6	NO.15	1 Bc7
NO.10	1 Be5	NO.13	1 PxP	NO.16	1 Qa1
NO.11	1 Pc3	NO.14	1 Qg1		

♛ 4 ♛

Black's Defenses

IN THE majority of modern two-movers the strategic interest arises from the character of black's defensive moves and the manner in which they influence white's mating moves. In many instances, as explained in the preceding chapter, the keymove may have no thematic connection with the strategy which the problem is composed to illustrate, so that the thematic content of the composition begins with black's moves. In this chapter various types of defensive moves will be described, beginning with those that are the least complex strategically.

In case of an attack perhaps the simplest defensive thing to do is to try to run away. So in a chess problem the simplest maneuver for black is to attempt to get his king out of danger by moving it. When there are a number of squares to which the king can move, these flight moves of the king may in themselves constitute the theme of the problem. Except as the achievement of a task, however, a position that merely emphasizes flights without connection with other strategic maneuvers is only mildly interesting. In actual composition it rarely is found practicable to combine any really complex strategy with several flight squares and the most attractive results are obtained in positions where the flights are limited to one or two. The largest percentage of modern two-movers have no flights, because flight squares may not be compatible with the theme that the composer is illustrating; yet whenever one or two flights are present they invariably have an agreeable effect. The introduction of a flight square into a problem is considered a meritorious feature, especially when the flight is not present in the initial position but is yielded by the key.

Examples of single flight squares made possible by the keymove have been shown in problems 1, 9, and 10, and in this chapter the key of No. 27 also yields a single flight. Problems 11, 13, 14, 22, and 23 have each a flight square in the initial position. Problem 8 has one flight square initially and the key gives a second one. No. 21 has two flight squares in the initial position, while the key of No. 20 gives two flights.

Whenever there is a flight square in the initial position of a problem it is desirable to have a mate already arranged should the black king move to that square. If there is a mate prepared for a certain black defense even before white makes the keymove it is spoken of as a *set mate*. If in a problem where the black king has a flight square in the initial position, there is no set mate prepared should the king move to that square, the king is said to have an *unprovided flight,* and this is regarded as a constructional defect. This is because that whenever a problem has a flight square, the first thing an experienced solver does is to look for a mate when the black king moves to that square. If no mate is provided, the solver at once seeks as a key a move which will permit a mate when the king moves. Thus an unprovided flight yields too strong a clue to the solution of the problem. There is an example of such an unprovided flight in problem 22, since there is no set mate in the initial position for 1 — — KxP.

17

Second Prize
Revue d' Echecs Tourney
1904

White mates in two moves

18

New York Evening Post
April 7, 1934

White mates in two moves

19

Grand Rapids Herald
May 12, 1935

White mates in two moves

20

Dagens Nyheder
October 30, 1932

White mates in two moves

After considering problems which feature flights for the black king, the next step in the strategic scale comprises positions where different black men move to defend the king against threatened mate, without there being any definite relationship among such defenses. A position of this kind is simply an assemblage of lines of play, and having no thematic elements it is regarded nowadays as of no problematic value. More interesting are positions in which several different mates follow various moves of a single black piece. This idea in itself may be considered as a theme. In problem 17, for example, each of the four possible moves of black's queen's knight defeats the threat and each leads to a different mate. Three of the moves of the king's knight also defeat the threat and lead to new mates.

In problem 18 white threatens mate by 2 Sf7 and black can only defend against this threat by moving the rook, so as to vacate the diagonal and let the queen's bishop guard f7. The various rook moves lead to several different types of thematic play which will be explained later, but the fact that the variations of the problem all arise from moves of the rook gives a thematic unity to the composition.

Instead of defending against a threat by attempts to guard his own king, in some positions black's defense may take the form of checks to the white king. White's replies to such checks are generically termed *counter-checks*, and they are divided into three types according to the manner in which white retorts. When the black checking piece is captured, and mate is given by the capturing piece, either directly or by discovery, it is a *direct-capture check*. When the white king moves out of the line of check and at the same time discovers mate from a white piece behind him it is a *royal battery check*. For such a check to effect mate the black checking man either must be a pawn or a piece which is pinned when it checks, so that it can not afterward interpose to defend the black king. The third type of counter-check is where a white man interposes between the black checking piece and the white king, and gives mate itself directly or discovers mate from another white piece. This third type is called a *cross-check*, because the white man "crosses" black's check.

Of these three types the direct-capture check is too simple and brutal to be attractive, and the royal battery check in most cases is too limited in its possibilities for any complex strategy. The cross-check is the most interesting strategically. In cross-check problems the thematic form of key is one that permits black checks which are not possible before the key is made. It is considered more essential from an artistic viewpoint to have thematic keys in cross-check problems than it is in those illustrative of many other themes.

Four problems are given in this chapter especially to illustrate various forms of cross-check composition. In problem 19 the white king himself moves to a square where he is exposed to a check by discovery from the black rook and to a direct check from the line-pinned black queen. A single battery is sufficient to counter both of these checks. In No. 20 the black king has no flights in the initial position, but the key, interfering with the lines of guard of two white pieces, gives two flights to the black king and a move to either flight square leads to a cross-check. Note that both the white knight and the black king have to move off the fifth rank to make these checks possible. This problem has two double batteries to deliver the mates, the bishop battery operating after the black checks, although in one case it functions as a single battery with a double check.

In the initial position of No. 21 the black king has two flight captures, which become checking moves after the key is made. In this case the black king again gives the checks by discovery. There is an additional cross-check when black plays 1 — — Rf5 ck, and there is also a direct-capture check following 1 — — Qe5 ck. While this is a cross-check problem, it was composed to illustrate three checks by discovery given by white's queen's pawn, viz., 1 Pg6, Sc5; 2 PxS: 1 — — KxKR ck; 2 Pd5: 1 — — Qe5 ck; 2 PxQ. White utilizes both a triple pawn battery and a single knight battery. All three of these problems have thematic keys, since in each case it is the keymove that makes the black checks possible.

In the initial position of the last of these four cross-check problems, No. 22, two cross-checks are set, viz., 1 — — Qb8 ck; 2 Se8, and 1 — — QxP ck; 2 Sd5. The theme of the problem is the replacing of white's replies to these checks with other mates. In other words the cross-checks are said to be changed. To do this white abandons the knight battery by playing 1 Qh3, threatening mate by 2 Re4. This move of the queen forms an indirect battery, since when the rook moves on the "e" file it opens the guard of the queen on c3 and d3. Now if black checks after the keymove has been made, white interposes the rook, discovering mate from the bishop: 1 — — Qb8 ck; 2 Re8, and 1 — — QxP; 2 Re6. Whatever difficulty the solver may have in finding the key will largely be occasioned by his hesitancy to give up the set cross-checks. As mentioned earlier in this chapter this problem has the defect of an unprovided flight, since there is no mate originally set for the flight capture, 1 — — KxP.

Cross-checks are also shown in a number of other problems in this volume, reproduced to illustrate other themes, since cross-checks often can be readily combined with

21

*First Prize
Informal Tourney
July–December, 1932
The Western Morning News
and Daily Gazette*

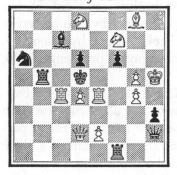

White mates in two moves

22

*American Chess Bulletin
January–February, 1939*

White mates in two moves

23

*The Western Morning News
and Mercury
August 27, 1927*

White mates in two moves

24

*The Pittsburgh Post
July 5, 1925*

White mates in two moves

other forms of strategy. In No. 52 there are three cross-checks resulting from moves of the black king. No. 43 has two discovered checks from the black king, countered by one double and one triple white battery. In No. 14 two discovered checks by a black pawn are countered by two single batteries. No. 50 has two direct checks by the black queen, met by a single bishop battery; and No. 58 has direct checks from two black pieces met by two batteries. In No. 57 there is one direct check and one by discovery. There are single cross-check variations in problems 68, 73, 77, and 84.

In the forms of strategy illustrated in modern two-movers the mutual interactions of the black men on each other have an exceedingly important role. This refers particularly to the manner in which the movement of a black man, in endeavoring to defend the black king, may affect the defensive powers of other black men.

In *Simple Two-Move Themes,* the 1924 volume of the *Christmas Series,* the general classification employed was based on the various types of motions of the chessmen "in their relations to the great principle of Obstruction (or rather in their three-fold relations to the absence of Obstruction, the removal of Obstruction, and the presence of Obstruction) and the book presents these types in order according as they appear in the keymove, in the black defenses, or in the white mates of the problem."

In defenses involving obstruction, the obstruction of a square is termed *square blocking,* or more simply *blocking,* and its converse is *square vacating.* The obstruction of a line is termed *interference* and its converse is *line-opening.* An interference can only affect the moves of a long-range piece—queen, rook or bishop—except that the double move of a pawn on its home rank may be interfered with by a man on the next rank, but otherwise any obstruction of a pawn move is a block. The knight may only be blocked, because it has no motion along a line. In the case of the king, obstruction is referred to as *self-blocking*, since the movement of the king can be obstructed only by a black man on an adjacent square. An interference can be occasioned by a man of either color, but blocking must be by a man of the same color as the man that is blocked, because the obstructing man would be liable to capture and the square on which it stood would not be blocked.

When an interference is by a man of one color on a man of another color, it is sometimes spoken of as a *shut-off*. This term is most commonly used where the interference is by a white man on a black one, particularly when it occurs on the mating move.

Self-blocks occur incidentally in connection with other features in literally thousands of problems, but they also may be made an important part of the thematic content of a problem, or a position may even be constructed just to illustrate self-blocking. Since self-blocking is one of the simplest forms of black maneuver some examples of it will be examined before more complex themes are considered.

As mentioned in Chapter Two there are three self-blocks in problem 1. The capture of the white rook, either by 1 — — QxR or by 1 — — BxR, blocks a· flight square, although giving the king a new one at c4. The third self-block, 1 — — RxP, makes it no longer necessary for white's queen's bishop to guard e5, and so permits mate by 2 Rd4. This is termed a white *self-interference mate;* the rook interfering with the bishop's guard on e5, that guard no longer being required. Illustrations of important self-blocks in connection with other strategy will be found in problem 10 in the variations 1 Be5, BxB (self-block); 2 QxR, and 1 — — SxB (self-block); 2 Rf4. Note also the main-play in problem 12, viz., 1 Rb6, RxP (self-block); 2 RxR.

Problems composed to illustrate self-blocks may have several unrelated self-blocks by different black men, but it is of greater thematic interest when one black man self-blocks on several squares. In No. 23 the black queen self-blocks on g6, g7, and g8 respectively. The effect, however, is somewhat blurred in this composition by the fact that 1 — — SxS and 1 — — Bg7 also are self-blocks that have the same result as does the movement of the queen to those squares. The problem would be more artistic if the self-blocking moves were only those made by the queen. Note that this problem has a Meredith setting and that the black king has a flight square in the initial position.

In No. 24, a waiting move position like No. 23, there are three self-blocks following the moves of black's queen's pawn, two of them resulting in self-interference mates by the knight, a device commonly employed by composers. This problem, however, was not composed merely to show these self-blocks, but to illustrate a variety of mates depending on moves of the black pawns. The movement of black's king's knight's pawn gives first an interference on the rook and then a line clearance for the white queen.

Another thematically interesting manner of treating self-blocks is to have different black pieces block the same square, with different ensuing mates. Six such self-blocks on a single square, followed by different mates, has been achieved, while eight is the task record in a two-mover for the maximum number of self-blocks on any squares with different mates (Appendix A2 and A3).

Problems may be composed specifically to show interference of one black piece on one or more other black pieces, as in No. 25, where the black rook interferes with the black queen and each of the bishops in turn, in the three thematic variations of the composition. In many problems a black knight interferes with several lines of guard of the long-range black pieces. An example is shown in problem 78. Here black's queen's knight interferes twice with the king's rook, once with the bishop, and twice with the queen, the interference on d7 being also an interference with the queen's rook.

An interference by a black bishop on a black rook, or vice versa, is termed a *Grimshaw interference* after a pioneer problem by the Yorkshire composer, Walter Grimshaw (*1832–1890*). In most positions, however, where there is to be such an interference, the composer arranges a mutual interference between the two pieces, with two different resulting mates, producing a *mutual Grimshaw*. In No. 26 this is illustrated in multiple form, the mutual interferences between the rooks and bishops occurring on four squares, b6, b7, c6, and c7. The arrangement of black rooks and bishops shown in this position has been employed in many problems. Loyd was fond of the arrangement, to which the fanciful appellation of "Organ Pipes" has been given. The element of originality in No. 26 lies in the combining of these multiple Grimshaw interferences with a white king battery. For an illustration of two separate mutual Grimshaw interferences combined in one position see problem 44.

Mutual Grimshaw interferences combine rather easily and effectively with other strategic elements. Of this fact problem 27 is a good illustration, such an interference taking place on c5. When the black rook, however, moves to c5 after 1 Qc6, the rook not only interferes with the black bishop's guard on b4, but it also interferes with the white queen's guard on c3 and at the same time it opens a line for the white queen to guard e4. Likewise, when the black bishop moves to c5, it interferes with the black rook's guard on b5 and also with the white queen's guard on c3, and at the same time it opens a line for the white rook to guard e4.

There is also an interference by the rook on the bishop when the rook moves to d6, but there is no corresponding effective interference by the bishop on the rook. Note, however, the complexity of this variation, 1 Qc6, Rd6 ck; 2 Be6. Four strategic elements are combined in the one black move, Rd6: an interference of the rook on the black bishop, a cross-check, and line openings both for the white bishop and white queen, the movement of the rook permitting the white bishop to play to e6 and parry the check, at the same time discovering mate from the white rook, since the line opening also permits the queen to guard the knight on e4. Constructively the position leaves considerable to be desired; both the awkward arrangement of the pawns and the use made of the black queen being objectionable.

In No. 28 the effective interferences between black's queen's rook and queen's bishop do not occur on the same square; the rook interferes with the bishop on b7, while the bishop interferes with the rook on d5. In an article in the April, 1940, issue of the *British Chess Magazine,* problem editor T. R. Dawson *(1889–1951)* termed such interferences on different squares *unit Grimshaws,* to distinguish them from Grimshaws where there is a mutual interference on the same square. Note when black plays the bishop to d5 it interferes with both rooks.

In problem 29 both the black rooks and the queen's bishop play to d5 in the thematic variations to interfere with the guard of the white bishop on e6, thus indirectly preventing the rook from mating at f7. 1 — — Bd5 interferes with both rooks, allowing 2 Qa1 mate. 1 — — QRd5

25

Entry in C. C. L. A. Tourney
1936 (C. C. L. A. Bulletin
October–November, 1937)

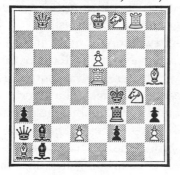

White mates in two moves

26

Fourth Prize
Revue d' Echecs Tourney
1904

White mates in two moves

27

First Prize
Second International Tourney
Newcastle Weekly Chronicle
July 10, 1926

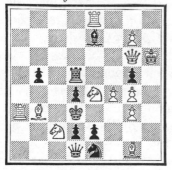

White mates in two moves

28

Entry in First Tourney
El Ajedrez Argentino
1926

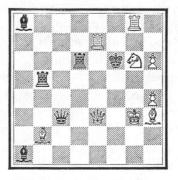

White mates in two moves

interferes with the black queen's bishop but opens the line of guard of the black queen on f1 so that white can mate only by 2 Se4. 1 — — KRd5 also interferes with the black queen's bishop but opens the diagonal for the king's bishop to pin the white knight on g3, so that the only mating move is 2 Se5, discovering check from the queen and at the same time shutting off the black bishop.

In an interference between two long-range men the square on which the interference occurs is termed the *critical square*. In a Grimshaw interference this square is vacant before the interference takes place. The interfering pieces normally are a rook and a bishop, but the queen may take the place of one of these pieces if she is line-pinned. When the queen is pinned she is said to be *line-pinned*, because she can always move along the line of pin, whether vertical, lateral or diagonal, but not off it. It is impossible to have the queen pinned so that she cannot move. A rook may be line-pinned along a rank or on a file, and a bishop may be line-pinned along a diagonal.

When a pawn is on its home square, so that it has the option of moving two squares, it may take the place of a rook in a mutual interference with a bishop. This special type of interference is termed a *pawn-Grimshaw*, and an example of it is shown in problem 46, where after 1 Se3, black in one of the thematic variations defends against the threat by 1 — — Pc6. Here the pawn interferes with the movement of the bishop along the diagonal and permits 2 Sb7 mate. The other mate of the Grimshaw pair occurs when black defends by 1 — — Bc6. Now the bishop interferes with the pawn and white mates by 2 BxR.

Where a white man is sacrificed on the critical square

the interference, instead of being a Grimshaw, is called a
Nowotny interference, after Anton Nowotny (1829–1871),
although other composers had shown the interference before Nowotny published an example of it in a four-mover
in the *Leipziger Illustrirte Zeitung,* April 29, 1854.

The Nowotny interference is illustrated in the threat line
of the three-mover, No. 136, in Chapter Twelve. The key
of this problem is 1 Pc5, with the threat of 2 Pc6, which
interferes with the lines of guard both of black's queen's
rook and queen's bishop, and threatens two mates, viz.,
2 Se6 and 2 QxPf3. 1 — — RxP prevents the first of these
mates but not the second, and 1 — — BxP prevents the
second mate but not the first. Any indifferent move by
black gives white a choice of these mates.

While such a dual threat is of common occurrence in
problems with a Nowotny interference, it is not an essential characteristic of the theme. In fact, in the four-mover
which gave Nowotny's name to the interference, no dual
mates are threatened. Problem 30 is also an example of
the Nowotny in which the move of a white man onto the
critical square does not set up a double threat.

In No. 136 the move 2 Pc6 makes possible threats of
mate by two other white men, but in No. 30 the knight
that makes the keymove threatens mate itself by 2 Sf4. Its
capture either by the black rook or bishop allows the
queen to mate. When 1 Sd3, RxS, the rook interferes with
the bishop's guard on f1 and permits mate by 2 Qf1. When
1 — — BxS, the bishop interferes with the rook's ability to
play to d7 and permits mate by 2 Qc8.

While Grimshaws are often seen in two-movers blended
with various other elements, such is not the case with the
Nowotny. One reason is that the key of a Nowotny two-
mover must be the move of a white man onto the interfer-

ence square, while a potential Grimshaw interference does not restrict the kind of key that may be used, making it easier to combine a Grimshaw with other elements.

The move of a black man may interfere with one line of movement of another black man and simultaneously open a second line of movement for that man. Again the moving black man may interfere with one black man and at the same time open a line for a third black man. In the first case two units are concerned; in the second case, three. The 1930 volume of the *Christmas Series* was devoted to an exposition of these themes and was entitled *Valves and Bi-Valves*. The *valve* involves one moving man and one stationary piece; the *bi-valve*, one moving man and two stationary pieces.

T. R. Dawson has conducted in the *British Chess Magazine* an elaborate study of this combined line opening and interference where the active man is a black pawn. He prefers, however, the use of the term *pawn-switch* for this maneuver as being more precisely descriptive than the term valve. An example of the pawn switch is shown in problem 31. The key is 1 Kh2, threatening 2 Sh1. The movement of black's queen's bishop's pawn opens the diagonal b8–h2 so that the black bishop pins the knight and prevents the threatened mate. 1 — — Pc6, while opening the line for the bishop, closes the line b6–f6, shutting off the black rook on b6, and permits white to mate by 2 Se5, which shuts off both the rook on b5 and the bishop. If 1 — — Pc5, the line b5–f5 is closed, shutting off the rook on b5, and white now mates by 2 Sd6, which shuts off both the other rook and the bishop.

A doubling of the theme is shown in No. 32. The key is 1 Kf8, threatening 2 Qe8. The moves of black's king's bishop's pawn open a line for the black queen to guard e8 and thus defeat the threat, but the pawn then inter-

29

Second Prize
Third Half-Yearly Tourney
Mid-week Sports Referee
July 8, 1926

White mates in two moves

30

Fourth Honorable Mention
Informal Meredith Tourney
The Falkirk Herald
March 23, 1927

White mates in two moves

31

Grand Rapids Herald
December 3, 1933

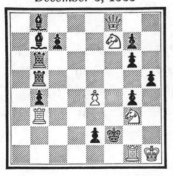

White mates in two moves

32

V. British Chess Magazine
July, 1934

White mates in two moves

feres with other lines of black guard, i. e., 1 —— Pf6; 2 KRxP, or 1 —— Pf5; 2 Se5. The effect of moving black's queen's bishop's pawn is more subtle. Instead of opening a line of guard, the moves of the pawn may be regarded as an anticipatory opening of a line for the black king, inasmuch as they provide a potential flight square, should white continue 2 Qe8 ck. 1 —— Pc5, however, interferes with the black queen's play along the rank and allows mate by 2 Ba4. 1 —— Pc6, while opening one potential flight for the black king closes another. In other words, it self-blocks c6 and permits the self-interference mate 2 Sb6.

This latter defense of black also acts as a switch on the white pieces, since while cutting off the guard on d6 by the white rook by closing the rank, it opens the diagonal for the white queen to guard that square. The author made a series of experiments with switch moves of black men affecting white pieces rather than black ones, and illustrations in three-move form are shown in problems 147 and 148 in Chapter Twelve.

SOLUTIONS

NO.17	1 Qa4	NO.22	1 Qh3	NO.27	1 Qc6
NO.18	1 Sg5	NO.23	1 Pg5	NO.28	1 KRg7
NO.19	1 Ke7	NO.24	1 Sh4	NO.29	1 Re7
NO.20	1 Sf6	NO.25	1 Sf6	NO.30	1 Sd3
NO.21	1 Pg6	NO.26	1 Sb4	NO.31	1 Kh2
		NO.32	1 Kf8		

5

Pinning and Unpinning

PINNING and unpinning have prominent roles in the modern problem, particularly in the two-mover. A man is *pinned* when it is on a line between its king and a long-range piece of the opposite color, so that it cannot move off the line because it would leave the king in check.

As mentioned in the last chapter, a queen when pinned always can move along the line of pin, and so she is said to be *line-pinned*. A rook or a bishop likewise will be line-pinned when it is pinned by a piece of similar motion. A pawn may be line-pinned vertically by a queen or rook on the same file and such pinning only prevents the pawn from making a capture. A pawn may be line-pinned diagonally under the conditions illustrated in problem 168 in Chapter Fourteen, where the pinned pawn makes an en passant capture by moving on the line of pin.

More attention has been given to the composing of problems showing the unpinning of white men than to those featuring black unpinning. So in this chapter the positions that will be examined first are those in which pinned white men are unpinned to enable them to give mate either directly or by discovery. In such problems the thematic type of key is one which pins the white man that is to be unpinned by black's defenses.

Black can unpin a white man either by interference, by moving another black man onto the line of pin, or by the withdrawal of the pinning piece. The illustrating of *interference unpins* has been much more popular with composers than that of *withdrawal unpins*. Problem 33 is a simple example of interference unpins. Opening with a thematic key, which pins the piece that is to be unpinned, there are two unpinning variations. When 1 —— Sc4, note that the knight interferes with both rooks.

Although the key of No. 34 is not thematic in regard to the unpinning play, it may be looked upon as thematic in that it makes possible the main-play of the problem, which is designed to show the combination of an en passant pawn capture with pawn promotions. The knight's pawn gives mate by promotion to queen or knight according as it is unpinned by the black pawn in making the en passant capture or by moves of the black knight.

More attention has been given to the unpinning of the white queen than to that of any other white piece, probably because the queen can deliver more mates when unpinned. A rook, bishop or knight can deliver only two such mates each, unless they give mate by discovery as in problem 40. The record for the queen is five different mates, when released either from an orthogonal or a diagonal pin. To show five unpins of the queen, however, is a difficult and complex task, and, as in other instances, more attractive results often may be attained when the theme is not pushed to its maximum limits. In Problem 35 the white queen is unpinned by the moves of four different black men to d6 to defeat the threatened mate, 2 Sb2, by cutting off the guard of the white bishop on b4. Each of these defenses leads to a different mate by the unpinned white queen. The line-pin mate, 1 —— Se7; 2 Qf4, should also be noted. The position was penalized by the judge be-

33

*Fourth and Fifth Prize
(ex aequo)
Informal Meredith Tourney
The Falkirk Herald
March 23, 1927*

White mates in two moves

34

*Second Honorable Mention
Informal Tourney
July–December, 1935
The Western Morning News
and Daily Gazette*

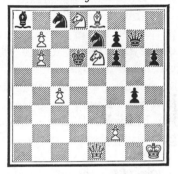

White mates in two moves

35

*Third Honorable Mention
Informal Tourney
January–June, 1936
The Western Morning News
and Daily Gazette*

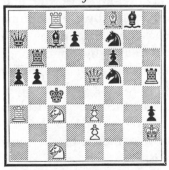

White mates in two moves

36

*The Western Morning News
and Daily Gazette
July 14, 1934*

White mates in two moves

cause of the major dual after 1 — — Sg3, an unwelcome unpin of the queen.

A combination of pinning and unpinning by a single black move is shown in No. 36 where black's two thematic defenses pin the knight that threatens mate and at the same time unpin the other white knight. The key is thematic since the white knight self-pins itself by a capture, but it is a key that will be seen quickly by the experienced solver because the knight is out of play in the initial position. The key of problem 37 also is thematic, but it has just the opposite effect to that of No. 36. Instead of pinning a white man it unpins one that already is pinned, allowing it to threaten mate. Such an unpinning key in itself, although thematic, would not be considered good because it plainly strengthens white's attacking powers. In this instance, however, it makes possible black's two thematic defenses, which re-pin the white bishop but simultaneously unpin the knight, allowing it to deliver two different mates.

So far the white unpins that have been examined are ones occasioned by the interference of black men on the pinning line. In the next three positions black unpins white by a withdrawal of the pinning piece. No. 38 is a simple illustration, the withdrawal moves of the black bishop leading to two different mates by the unpinned white queen. In No. 39 the black rook unpins the white bishop, leading to two different mates by double-check depending upon the rook's withdrawal move. In problem 40 there are three thematic lines following withdrawal unpins by the black queen. Note that the queen self-blocks in two of these variations, viz., 1 — — Qd4; 2 Re6, and 1 — — QxKP; 2 Rd5. Certain other moves of the queen lead to the third unpin mate, 2 RxP.

Problem 41 shows the interference unpinning of two

37

*The Western Morning News
and Mercury
January 9, 1926*

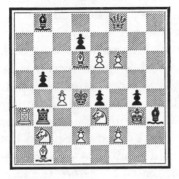

White mates in two moves

38

*Honorable Mention
Third Quarter, 1928
Die Schwalbe
July, 1928*

White mates in two moves

39

*The Chess Amateur
August, 1927*

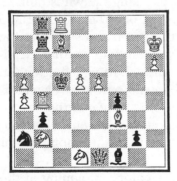

White mates in two moves

40

*Commended
Second Half-Yearly Informal
Tourney
Bristol Times and Mirror
March 27, 1926*

White mates in two moves

white pieces by the defensive moves of one black piece, which makes three unpinning moves altogether. The next position, No. 42, was composed to show the unpinning of either of two white pieces by the withdrawal of one or the other of the black pinning pieces.

Finally in No. 43 a position appears where no pinning of white occurs at all because the key is an anticipatory preventive of it. White wants to threaten mate by 2 Sd4, and in order to do this the bishop must vacate that square. White must not, however, move the bishop to a square from which it will not guard the f6 square after 1 —— KxRe6 ck; 2 Sf3. Accordingly the bishop will have to retreat along the d4–a1 diagonal. Should the bishop go to c3 or a1 black would reply 1 —— Ra2, pinning the knight so it could not mate. Therefore the keymove is 1 Bb2, making 1 —— Ra2 ineffectual.

The next three positions are examples of problems in which there is an unpinning of a black man as a defensive measure. When this occurs in a two-mover the purpose of unpinning the black man is so it can directly guard against a threatened mate. In problem 44 the key is 1 Sb4, threatening mate by 2 Qd3, since black's king's pawn is pinned. The movement of either black rook or either black bishop onto the king's file will unpin this pawn and so defeat the threat. These thematic defenses result in mutual Grimshaw interferences both on e5 and e6, to which attention has already been called in Chapter Four. In a classification of this problem according to its principal theme, the double mutual Grimshaw undoubtedly would be considered a more important feature than the unpinning of the pawn.

In problem 45 there is an anticipatory unpinning of the black rook. This rook is pinned in the initial position, but it is unpinned by the thematic key, 1 Sc2, which sets up a

41

*The Observer
June 18, 1932*

White mates in two moves

42

*Grand Rapids Herald
April 21, 1934*

White mates in two moves

43

*Dagens Nyheder
January 14, 1934*

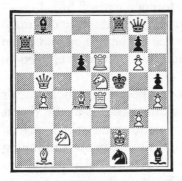

White mates in two moves

44

*First Highly Commended
22nd International Tourney
Brisbane Courier
November 13, 1926*

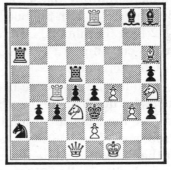

White mates in two moves

masked battery. White threatens to play 2 Se3, when the bishop will again be pinning the rook. To forestall this pin black can move either the knight or bishop to e4, similarly as white plays 1 Bb2 in problem 43 to prevent the subsequent pinning of a white piece. The movement either of the knight or bishop opens a line for the white queen and leads to a half-pin mate, a term which will be discussed in the next chapter. It may be interesting for the reader to note that in this problem the following strategic elements are combined: unpinning of black by white; threatened mate from a masked battery; anticipatory prevention of pinning; black line opening for white, doubled; and half-pin mating positions, doubled.

White threatens mate in No. 46 by 1 Se3 and 2 SxS. Black can guard the knight on c4 either by an interference unpin of the knight on b6 or the rook on b4. This can be accomplished by 1 — — Pc6 and 1 — — Pc5 respectively. 1 — — Bc6 also unpins the knight on b6. 1 — — Pc6 self-blocks that square and so permits white to mate by the self-interference move 2 Sb7. 1 — — Pc5 also is a self-block, permitting the self-interference mate 2 Sf5. 1 — — Bc6 interferes with the black pawn so that white can mate by 2 BxR. The mutual interference of the bishop and pawn on c6 constitutes a pawn-Grimshaw, already referred to in Chapter Four.

Two-movers also have been composed in which black's thematic defenses unpin a black man to defeat the threat and at the same time unpin a white man which mates. Problems 47 and 48 show tripled simultaneous unpinning of the black and white queens. In No. 47 both queens are pinned diagonally. Tripled simultaneous unpinning of both queens in an orthogonal setting has been shown by the Italian composer Alberto Mari *(1892–1953)* and later by the author, in a somewhat more economical

45

The Falkirk Herald
April 21, 1926

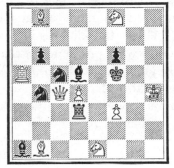

White mates in two moves

46

The Observer
November 17, 1935

White mates in two moves

47

V. American Chess Bulletin
January–February, 1939

White mates in two moves

48

V. American Chess Bulletin
March–April, 1941

White mates in two moves

version. Since then the American two-move specialist, Frederick Gamage *(1882–1957)*, succeeded in doing it with a flight square.

In No. 48 the black queen is pinned laterally and the white queen diagonally. When the white queen is unpinned she administers mate at a distance of one or two squares from the black king, which is more attractive than are mates on squares adjacent to the king, as in No. 47. It may be noted in connection with problem 48, that in 1923 the Canadian composer, Jacob E. Funk (*b. 1889*), published a position showing quadrupled simultaneous unpinning of a diagonally pinned white queen and a laterally pinned black *bishop* (Appendix A4).

SOLUTIONS

NO.33	*1* Kf4	NO.38	*1* Bf1	NO.43	*1* Bb2
NO.34	*1* Pf4	NO.39	*1* Qh4	NO.44	*1* Sb4
NO.35	*1* Sd3	NO.40	*1* Se1	NO.45	*1* Sc2
NO.36	*1* SxP	NO.41	*1* Re8	NO.46	*1* Se3
NO.37	*1* Pf4	NO.42	*1* Be8	NO.47	*1* Sc1
		NO.48	*1* SxQP		

6

Black Self–Pinning

IN THE last chapter examples were shown of problems in which white self-pinned one of his men by a thematic keymove. This occurred in No. 33 and in No. 36. In this chapter various forms of black self-pinning will be considered. Black may self-pin a man in four different ways: (1) by capturing a white man on a line between the black king and a long-range white piece; (2) by the movement of the black king himself; (3) by the interposition of a black man on a line of check, which in a two-mover would necessitate a checking key; (4) by the withdrawal of a black man from a potential line of pin, leaving a second black man pinned, which is what takes place in half-pinning problems.

The self-pinning of a black man occurs in many problems as a secondary or incidental feature. To constitute the principal theme of a composition the self-pinning should be repeated in two or more variations, as in No. 49. In this problem a black knight self-pins itself by capture in two variations, and in a third the knight is self-pinned by a move of the black king.

Problem 50 shows two self-pins of the black queen by capture combined with several other strategic features. The thematic keymove, 1 Ba3, self-pins white's king's

bishop. Black's two thematic defenses, 1 — — QxQBP ck
and 1 — — QxKBP ck, simultaneously unpin this bishop,
check the white king and self-pin the black queen. The
unpinned bishop then delivers cross-check mates.

No. 51 was composed to produce three self-pins of the
queen by moves of the black king. In No. 52 two self-pins
of this type occur in conjunction with cross-checking play,
the problem being composed primarily to feature cross-
checks. The key, 1 Pe6, is thematic in that it permits the
black checks and also makes possible one of the black
self-pins of the rook by a move of the black king. The
self-pinning variations are 1 — — Kd6 ck; 2 Qe5, and 1
— — Kc4 ck; 2 Se5.

The third type of self-pinning, that by the interposition
of a black man on the line of a check, is merely of aca-
demic interest in a two-mover, since no problem would
be composed nowadays with a checking key, unless specifically designed to show some such defense which could
be illustrated in no other way.

The fourth manner in which a black man may be self-
pinned is by the withdrawal of one black man from a potential line of pin leaving a second black man pinned.
This may occur whenever two black men are located on
a line between the black king and a long-range white
piece, i. e., queen, rook or bishop. In such a setting each
of the two black men is potentially or "one-half" pinned,
and the term *half-pin* was given to this arrangement by
the two-move specialist, Comins Mansfield *(b. 1896)*, in his
correspondence with Murray Marble *(1885-1919)* during
1915. In what are termed *complete half-pins* whichever
man is left pinned, by the movement of its fellow, could
prevent the ensuing mate were it not for the pin, so that the
mate is a *pin-mate.* In other words, in a complete half-pin

49

V. American Chess Bulletin
January–February, 1940

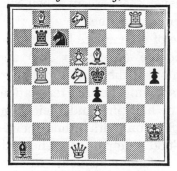

White mates in two moves

50

American Chess Bulletin
September–October, 1938

White mates in two moves

51

American Chess Bulletin
January–February, 1940

White mates in two moves

52

V. Chess Review
March, 1933

White mates in two moves

there is a pin-mate resulting from the move of either black man off the line of pin. When a pin-mate occurs after the withdrawal of one of the pair but not after that of the other, the half-pin is said to be *incomplete*. It is not customary today to compose incomplete half-pins and in modern two-movers they practically are never seen except when incidental to the illustration of some other theme.

The earliest known example of a complete half-pin was composed in 1855 by A. Kempe (Appendix A5) and within the following decade most of the more simple permutations of the theme were shown. The true realization, however, of the possibilities of half-pins and their wonderful development in combination with other themes dates from the work of the Good Companions. The half-pin is now one of the most common elements in two-movers, probably because of the ease with which it can be combined with other strategic elements, such as self-blocks, line openings, unpins and cross-checks. Half-pins are known as *homogeneous* when the pinned pairs are the same kind of men, as in problems 53, 55, and 59; *heterogeneous* when the pairs are composed of men of different kinds, as in problems 54, 56, 57, 58, and 60.

No. 53 shows a complete, homogeneous half-pin in a Meredith setting. The key is a waiting move, 1 Rf2. If 1 — — Bb4; 2 Pc3. If 1 — — Bb5; 2 Pc4. If 1 — — Bb3; 2 PxB. In each case the bishop remaining on the rook's file is self-pinned by the withdrawal of its fellow and the ensuing mates are pin-mates. Problem 54 has three half-pinned heterogeneous pairs of black men. A similar problem has since been composed with three homogeneous pairs (Appendix A6). No. 55 was composed to show a duel between the white and black pawns, viz., 1 Bc7, Pg6; 2 Pe3, and 1 — — Pg5; 2 Pe4. The half-pin is merely incidental, which is explained by the date of the composi-

53

The Falkirk Herald
September 23, 1925

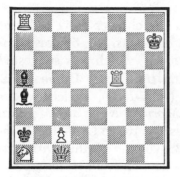

White mates in two moves

54

Second Prize
Antony Guest Memorial
Tourney
The Falkirk Herald
July 29, 1925

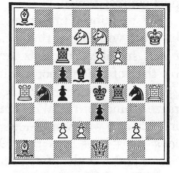

White mates in two moves

55

American Chess Bulletin
November, 1904

White mates in two moves

56

Mid-week Sports Referee
October 21, 1926

White mates in two moves

tion, since at that time the author had not become interested in half-pins. If black, however, plays 1 — — Bg5, then 2 Pe3 is a true half-pin mate, and if 1 — — Bg6 or f5; then 2 Pe4. Despite its crude construction, the author has thought best to reproduce this position, exactly as it was composed, as a specimen of his earlier efforts in complex composition.

The remaining problems in this chapter show half-pins blended with other thematic elements. No. 56 was composed specifically for its keymove, which was suggested by that of a joint composition by George Hume (*1862-1936*) and Duncan Pirnie (*1885-1959*), which was a prize winner in the *Western Morning News and Mercury* in 1922 and was reproduced as No. 109 in *Changing Fashions*. This book was the 1925 volume of the *Christmas Series* and was devoted to a selection from Hume's problems. For the last twenty years of his life Hume was the custodian of the great collection of problems that Alain White had begun to gather many years previously and Hume also edited those volumes of White's *Christmas Series* which were published from 1915 to 1935. In problem 56 the key is 1 Kg7, releasing the rook from the diagonal pin by the bishop but subjecting it to a lateral pin by the queen. Yet though the rook is pinned laterally it can move along the line of pin, so that after the keymove it threatens 2 Re7 mate.

In problems 57 and 58 half-pins are blended with cross-checks. The thematic variations in the former are 1 KxP, RxS ck; 2 Qf6, and 1 — — Se3 ck; 2 Se6. Black gives one direct check and one check by discovery. This probably is the easiest way to produce the two cross-checks. In No. 58 both black checks are direct: 1 KxBP, BxS ck; 2 Se5, and 1 — — Qf3 ck; 2 Sf5. The classic illustration of the combination of half-pins with direct checks by both black

57

American Chess Bulletin
November–December, 1939

White mates in two moves

58

The Western Morning News
and Daily Gazette
October 16, 1937

White mates in two moves

59

Skakbladet
May, 1934

White mates in two moves

60

Skakbladet
October, 1934

White mates in two moves

men is a problem by Alain White (Appendix A7) with only ten men! The keys to No. 57 and No. 58 may be regarded as thematic in that they make possible black's checks, although the employment of capture keys was an unpleasing necessity. The thematic key for a half-pin would be the movement of the white pinning piece onto the line of pin, but this usually is too "strong" a move to be desirable for a key unless there are offsetting features. White's problem has such a key, but in its case the key makes possible the black checks. This fact redeems the character of the key and also makes it doubly thematic.

Problem 59 combines a half-pin with a *half-battery*. In a half-battery there are two white men on a line between the black king and an attacking long-range white piece. If a black man captures either of the two intervening white men, the other one of the white pair moves off the line and checks the black king, leaving the black man pinned that made the capture, so that it cannot interpose or capture the checking piece. In the combination of half-pin and half-battery in No. 59 both black rooks are thematically pinned in the two theme variations. 1 Qa8, threat 2 Qe8. 1 — — RxR; 2 Sc3. 1 — — RxS; 2 Rc4.

In No. 60 there are two highly elaborated variations, the play in one echoing that in the other. Positions of this character are often called *dithemes* and are especially popular at the present time. The thematic play in this particular problem is a blending of half-pins with self-pins, followed by white shut-offs of black. The key is 1 Qh4, with the threat of 2 Sd4. In the two thematic variations black defends by capturing one or the other of the knights. 1 — — QxS, self-pinning the queen by capture and the bishop by withdrawal; 2 Sd6, shutting off the black bishop. 1 — — BxS, self-pinning the bishop by capture and the queen by withdrawal; 2 Se7, shutting off the black rook.

SOLUTIONS

NO.49	1 Re8	NO.53	1 Rf2	NO.57	1 KxP
NO.50	1 Ba3	NO.54	1 Qe2	NO.58	1 KxBP
NO.51	1 SxP	NO.55	1 Bc7	NO.59	1 Qa8
NO.52	1 Pe6	NO.56	1 Kg7	NO.60	1 Qh4

7

The Mating Move

IN MANY two-movers the keymove, some of black's defenses and the ensuing mating moves all play a part in the theme that is being illustrated. In other problems the interest may lie chiefly in only two of these moves. The keymove and black's defenses may make up the thematic content of the problem, the mating moves in themselves being uninteresting; or a problem may be composed to show certain black maneuvers and the resulting mates, the composer providing the best key that he can after the position is otherwise completed. Again the chief feature of a composition may lie in just one of these moves. Some problems are composed to show striking keymoves; others to illustrate strategic black defenses. Likewise there are two-movers composed primarily for white's mating moves.

Interesting types of mating moves have been shown in some of the problems in previous chapters. Problems 5, 12, 13, and 27 are instances of compositions in which the mating moves in the main-plays are of particular interest because they form an essential part of a striking theme. In cross-checking problems the manner in which white defends against black's checks and simultaneously delivers mate make white's mating moves of predominant interest in most instances. Shut-offs of black pieces by the mating moves were illustrated in the last chapter in problems 53, 55, and 60.

In this present chapter the illustrations are confined to compositions in which the mating moves are the outstanding feature. No. 61, for example, shows a white rook effecting mate by playing to seven different squares. In this position it is the moves of the rook that are of dominant interest, rather than the black moves that determine them. The rook, operating as the firing piece of a battery can be made to play to a maximum of fourteen different squares in a two-mover. A task problem of this kind, however, is rarely attractive because many of the mates will necessarily be so similar in character that the general effect is uninteresting. In a problem, featuring the play of one piece, where no effort is made even to approach maximum possibilities, each individual mate can be made more distinctive, as is the case in No. 61.

A white knight, firing a battery, can deliver mate on a maximum of eight squares. This task is known as a *white knight wheel.* Here again the most attractive results frequently are obtained where the composer does not attempt to force the maximum number of mates. Although in No. 62 the knight gives only five mates, each one has some individual strategic interest. A partial *black knight wheel* is shown in problem 78.

No. 63 was composed primarily to show the self-interference mates by the moves of the queen's pawn, following the self-blocking defenses 1 — — Bf5 and 1 — — Pf6, though secondary features were added, such as the two mates by the queen's knight, that after the third self-block, 1 — — Sf5, also being a self-interference. In No. 64 the pawn interferences on the black queen are interesting, but it is the long-range mating moves of the white queen that give the position its attractiveness. These particular mates were shown in a problem by Gamage that won first prize in *Tidskrift för Schack* in 1911, and so this combination of black and white play is termed the Gamage theme. No. 64 was constructed to show these mates in as light a setting as possible.

The next three problems feature mate by pawn promotions. In No. 65 a white pawn promotes to a knight on two adjacent squares in the thematic variations. In No. 66 the threat is a pawn promotion to a knight, and in the variation play there are pawn promotions to queen on three adjacent squares, d8, e8, and f8. Note that in each of these three cases the promotion must be to a queen, since a promotion to rook or bishop will not suffice. Finally problem 67 shows pawn promotions either to knight or queen, both on e8 and on g8 according to black's play. Of course the self-blocks by the black knights add considerably to the interest of this position, but nevertheless the mating moves are the principal feature.

Black has four different defensive moves in No. 68, none of which can be played before the key is made, and the resulting mate in each case is by a double-check. The mate after 1 — — QB moves, ck, is the same as in the threat, except that after black's check the mate is by double-check. The theme of this problem is mate by double-check and consequently it would spoil the thematic unity of the composition to have any variation in which a double-check would not be required.

61

*Solving Contest
Marshall Chess Club
House Opening
December 19, 1931*

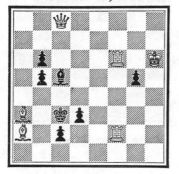

White mates in two moves

62

*The Western Morning News
and Mercury
October 10, 1931*

White mates in two moves

63

*American Chess Bulletin
January, 1936*

White mates in two moves

64

*American Chess Bulletin
November–December, 1939*

White mates in two moves

65

American Chess Bulletin
July–August, 1935

White mates in two moves

66

Skakbladet
April, 1934

White mates in two moves

67

The Observer
November 15, 1925

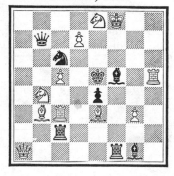

White mates in two moves

68

British Chess Magazine
December, 1926

White mates in two moves

SOLUTIONS

NO.61 *1* Qh8   NO.64 *1* Bg5   NO.67 *1* Qc3

NO.62 *1* Rb4–a4   NO.65 *1* Qh1   NO.68 *1* Bg5

NO.63 *1* Sf8   NO.66 *1* Rb8

8

Complex Themes

THE MAJORITY of modern two-movers show several thematic elements in combination and the tendency is for such blends to become increasingly complex as composers search continually for novel effects. In this chapter a few examples of theme combinations are given to illustrate how complex they may become.

The play in the first position, No. 69, is not very intricate. It does involve, however, a couple of self-blocks combined with line openings for the white queen, following a flight-sacrifice keymove that shuts off what looks like a white battery but which never functions as such. The two thematic variations are 1 Rd4, SxR; 2 Qb8, and 1 — — BxR; 2 QxQ.

In the two thematic variations in No. 70, the play in one is an echo of that in the other, so that the composition may be classed as a ditheme, like problem 60. The key is 1 Rc3, threatening 2 RxBP. Black can guard this pawn with either the knight or the bishop, but in each case the move interferes with the guard of black's king's rook on the king's pawn. When the black's rook's guard is shut off white threatens to mate by capturing black's king's pawn with the king's rook or with the queen. 1 — — Se5, however, pins white's rook (by withdrawal) so that the capture has to be made with the queen, whereas 1 — — Be6 pins the queen (by withdrawal) so that only the rook can administer mate. These two defenses illustrate dual avoidance. Black's moves are also examples of bi-valve play, since in interfering with the guarding power of one black piece they simultaneously release the pinning power of other black pieces. The problem has three other variations which are merely incidental and unthematic.

As previously mentioned, certain forms of maneuvers, such as Grimshaw and Nowotny interferences, have been named after the composers who first illustrated them. Many themes, especially in the two-move field, have similarly been named after the composers who first called attention to them. This practice is deprecated by some of the leading problem authorities on the ground that such names are not descriptive and are meaningless unless the reader already is familiar with the themes. There is considerable point to this argument, especially in view of the great number of themes that have been so named in recent years. A few years ago a prominent chess journal ran a long article explaining the various two-move themes which have been designated by composers' names. No attempt will be made here to cover even the more prominent of these themes, but a few examples will be given merely as illustrations.

Problems 71 and 72 show the *Dalton theme*, named after the American composer, Dr. W. R. Inge Dalton (*1841–1931*). In this theme a white piece unpins a black one and then that white piece is in turn pinned by a move of the piece that it has unpinned. The key to No. 71 is 1 Qe7, unpinning the black knight. Any move of the knight pins the queen by opening the battery, and so prevents the threatened mate, 2 Qc5. In No. 72 the principal variation, while based on the Dalton theme, is highly

69

Third Prize
First Tourney of
National Chess Federation
of U. S. A., 1928

White mates in two moves

70

The Pittsburgh Post
November 28, 1926

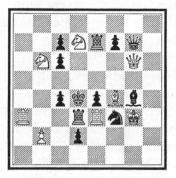

White mates in two moves

71

Honorable Mention
Informal Tourney
January–June, 1927
The Western Morning News
and Mercury

White mates in two moves

72

V. Bristol Times and Mirror
August 28, 1926

White mates in two moves

elaborated by the addition of other elements. The key is
1 Qg3, unpinning black's king's knight. This move also results in a self-pin of white's queen's knight. White now
threatens mate by 2 Qg7. Any move of the unpinned
knight will line-pin the queen on the diagonal (Dalton
theme) and prevent this mate. A general move of the
knight, however, permits the queen to mate by capturing
the pinning bishop, 2 QxB. The knight has two correcting
moves to prevent this mate. The first is 1 — — Se6, a self-
block leading to a self-interference mate, 2 Rf7. The other
correcting move is 1 — — Sg2. Observe what this move
does. 1. It line-pins the white queen by opening the diagonal for the bishop at d6. 2. It cuts off the white rook's potential guard on g5, so that 2 QxB is not mate. 3. It unpins
the white knight that was self-pinned by the keymove.
4. It interferes with the guard on the e4 square by the
bishop on h1. This single move of the knight simultaneously affects the powers of three other black pieces and
of three white pieces.

The Schiffmann defense is named after the brilliant
Roumanian composer, J. A. Schiffmann (*1904–1930*),
who died at twenty-six. In this theme white threatens a
mate by a discovered check from a battery, and in order
to prevent this mate black self-pins one of his men in such
a way that if white endeavors to carry out the threat the
firing piece of the white battery will unpin the self-pinned
black man and it will prevent the mate.

This theme has already been shown in problem 14 in
the variation 1 Qg1, PxS. Now the threat move, 2 Pf4,
does not mate, because the white pawn, which is the
firing piece of the battery, by its interference on the rook
at h4 has unpinned the black pawn, so that the black
pawn can interpose on the line of check. The Schiffmann
defense also appears in problem 62 in the variation 1 Rb4

73

*Solving Contest
Marshall Chess Club
House Opening
December 19, 1931*

White mates in two moves

74

*The Observer
July 13, 1941*

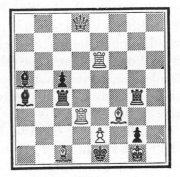

White mates in two moves

75

*American Chess Bulletin
July–August, 1941*

White mates in two moves

76

*American Chess Bulletin
January–February, 1949*

White mates in two moves

–a4, SxP. Here if the white knight, the firing piece of the battery, makes the threat move 2 Sb4, it unpins the black knight so that the latter can defend against the discovered check from the bishop.

No. 73 shows a doubling of the Schiffmann defense. The keymove is 1 Ke3, threatening 2 Sf7. If black, however, captures the king's pawn either with his knight or his bishop, white cannot proceed with 2 Sf7, since it would unpin the black piece; accordingly he has to play 2 RxP or 2 QxR respectively. Note that black could defend against these mates by interposition were it not for the pin. This pin-mate feature is desirable, if not essential, in this theme.

The black king has two flight squares in No. 73, and the white knight plays to four different squares in the various lines, delivering all the mates but the two in the thematic variations. This problem also shows a combination of direct and indirect batteries, which were explained in Chapter One. In the initial position the knight and queen form a direct battery aimed at the black king, and the knight and bishop form an indirect battery aimed at the square c5. Both of these batteries become effective in the threat line, 2 Sf7. When black plays 1 — — Kc5, however, the action of the batteries is transposed, the knight and bishop becoming a direct battery, and the knight and queen an indirect one.

The theme of No. 74 was suggested to the author by the Schiffmann defense, but it is essentially different, since in the thematic lines of play it is not the firing piece of a white battery that would unpin the self-pinned black man. In No. 74 mate is threatened by a direct check, instead of by a discovered check as in the Schiffmann defense. The threatened mate is prevented by the thematic defenses because white's move would be on the line of pin between a line-pinned black piece and the black king. This theme may be more readily understood by examining the actual play in No. 74. The key is 1 Pe4, threatening 2 Re3. There are two thematic defenses, 1 — — QRxP, and 1 — — KRxP. Although in each case the capturing piece becomes line-pinned, it could capture the white rook if white continued 2 Re3 ck. In each variation, however, the self-pinning defense permits white to administer a pin-mate, viz., 1 — — QRxP; 2 QxB, and 1 — — KRxP; 2 Qh4. In Problem 75 the same theme is illustrated with line-pinning of two black pieces on a diagonal instead of on a file.

In problem 76 black defeats the threat by square-vacating to prevent a capture by a pawn, discovering mate. This theme is shown with a lateral pawn battery in No. 17, where the threat is 2 PxS, and with a vertical pawn battery in No. 13, threatening 2 PxP.

No. 77 is an example of the Larsen theme, named after the Danish composer, K. A. K. Larsen (*b. 1896*). In his column in the London *Observer*, Brian Harley commented on this composition as follows: "The Larsen Theme is a variation-complex in which the black move does three things: (a) it unpins a black unit which then defeats the threat (b) it unpins a white unit which delivers mate (c) it checks the white king. In [No. 77] P–K5 unpins a black knight, so that it protects the rook; it unpins the white knight on queen's third, and discloses checks from the rook. I believe this example to be the first without a double-check mate in the thematic variation." Note that the keymove self-pins the white knight on d3, pins the black knight, and makes possible the black check.

Problem 78 illustrates the Schór theme, named after the Hungarian composer, L. Schór (*b. 1897*). In this theme white's keymove unpins a black man and simultaneously self-pins the keypiece; then the unpinned black

man in turn unpins the keypiece, enabling it to deliver
mate. There are two thematic lines in this position, 1
QxBP, Sf3; 2 Qd6, and 1 — — Sf7; 2 Qd4. There is also a
third unpin of the queen by the other black knight, 1 — —
Sf5; 2 Qe4. In this problem the Schór theme is blended
with a partial black knight wheel, the moves of the knight
on e5 producing six distinct variations. The author was
responsible for the queen unpins, while Mr. Harley
elaborated the other defenses of the queen's knight. In the
course of its composition this problem made several
journeys back and forth over the Atlantic before both
composers were satisfied with the setting.

This particular problem may be used to explain what is
meant by the terms *fringe piece* and *fringe variation*.
These were of fairly common occurrence in the last century, but now are rarely seen in the work of good composers. A fringe piece is one that is not essential to the
problem from a constructional or thematic point of view,
but which is used to produce an additional, or fringe, variation, or is used merely to complicate one of the necessary
variations. If a man is actually a fringe piece it can be
removed without affecting the soundness or the thematic
content of the position. Sometimes a pair of men, one
white and one black, constitute a fringe, and both can be
removed without impairing the problem. In No. 78 the
knight on g7 is not constructionally necessary and although its use was originally suggested by the author, he
later questioned whether it might not be regarded as a
fringe piece and be removed. Mr. Harley, however, in-
sisted that it be retained since it effected a third unpin of
the white queen, and because of this he did not regard it
as extraneous to the theme of the problem.

The next two positions are examples of the *Howard
theme*. No. 79 shows the original form of this theme. A

77

The Observer
August 23, 1931

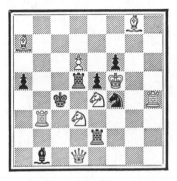

White mates in two moves

78

The Observer
August 9, 1925
with the collaboration
of Brian Harley

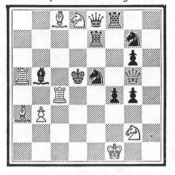

White mates in two moves

79

Dedication Problem
Georgio Guidelli Memorial
Tourney, L' Alfiere di Re
October–November, 1925
with the collaboration
of Alain White

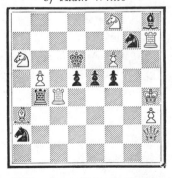

White mates in two moves

80

The Empire Review
January, 1926

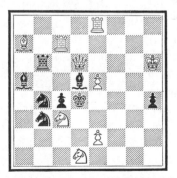

White mates in two moves

line-pinned white piece by moving along the line of pin and interfering with another white piece unpins a black man, which in turn unpins the white keypiece allowing it to mate. The key to this problem is 1 Rf4, unpinning black's king's pawn; black then plays 1 — — Pe4 unpinning the white rook; and white mates by 2 RxBP. The author originated the thematic play in this composition and Mr. White suggested the mutate setting.

Problem 80 is a modification of the theme in that white's keymove unpins a black man by the direct withdrawal of the white piece along its line of pin, instead of by an interference with another white piece. Here the theme is doubled since black has two thematic defenses: 1 Qf6, threat 2 Pe6; 1 — — Bc6; 2 Qf2, and 1 — — Be6; 2 Qf4. As mentioned in Chapter One, this problem is notable for a *thematic try*, which is a try that embodies the type of thematic play that the problem is constructed to illustrate. The try is 1 Qg6, with threats of 2 Pe3 and 2 Sb5. If 1 — — Bc6, unpinning the queen, then 2 Qg1, and if 1 — — Be6; 2 Qe4. It is of especial interest that, although these defenses unpin the white queen, they lead to mates on different squares than those in the actual solution. The only black defense which defeats this try is 1 — — Be4.

In 1921 George Hume composed a problem blending a half-pin with unpins of white that was awarded a prize in the problem tourney of the Eighth American Chess Congress (Appendix A8). This problem was published as No. 84 in *Changing Fashions* with the following remarks in the notes: "The Hume Theme derived its name from this position. The task involves two pinned white pieces, each to be unpinned in turn by an interference move made by one of two black half-pinned pieces, leading to true half-pin mates by the unpinned white men."

81

*The Observer
December 26, 1927*

White mates in two moves

82

*First Prize Two-Mover
First Quarter, 1929
Die Schwalbe
February, 1929*

White mates in two moves

83

*V. Third Honorable Mention
Second International Tourney
Skakbladet
December, 1931*

White mates in two moves

84

*Third Prize
Seventh Tourney
The Grantham Journal
July 1, 1933*

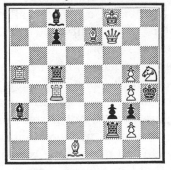

White mates in two moves

A year later, in *The Western Morning News and Mercury*, Hume in collaboration with C. S. Kipping (*1891-1964*) published a problem which is shown as No. 107 in *Changing Fashions*. On this composition Mr. White comments in the notes: "This is a new thematic blend, which we can helpfully call The Inverted Hume Theme. . . . The black half-pin is here, but instead of white unpinning, we get white pinning."

Problems 81 and 82 are examples of the *Inverted Hume theme*. In the former the key is 1 Qd4, threatening 2 QxPb2. Black has two thematic defenses. 1 —— Sc4 guards the pawn on b2 but self-pins the pawn on b4. It also pins the white knight on c7, so that white cannot play 2 Sb5 but must mate by 2 Qc3, since an incidental feature of the black knight's move is an interference on the black bishop. Black's second thematic defense is 1 —— Pb3, preventing the threat mate by pinning the queen. This move, however, also self-pins the black knight so that white now mates by 2 Sb5. This second variation also illustrates the Dalton theme; the white queen unpinning the black pawn and the latter then pinning the queen by opening a line for the black rook.

In No. 82 a pair of half-pinned black knights take the place of the half-pinned knight and pawn in No. 81. The key of No. 82 is 1 Rb8, threatening 2 Qb7. Any move of black's queen's knight pins the white queen, but also self-pins black's king's knight, allowing mate by 2 Sb4. 1 —— Sc5 also defeats the threat and at the same time pins the white knight, but it self-pins black's queen's knight, and incidentally interferes with black's king's bishop, so that white can mate by 2 QxP.

Problem 83 was composed to illustrate a change of pin of one black piece to another, caused by moving the black king. White plays 1 KSd5, threatening 2 Qe7, black's king's knight being pinned. Black defends against this threat by 1 — — Ke6, unpinning the knight. This move, however, self-pins black's other knight and white retorts 2 Qe4. Since this single line of play is hardly sufficient in itself for a problem, secondary defenses are added by arranging a line of guard to be opened on e7 by moves of black's queen's knight. The moves of this knight provide an example of correction play, which was described in connection with problem 6. If the knight makes a general move (to c4, b7, c8, e8 or f7) it opens the line of white's queen's rook to guard e6, so that white can mate by 2 Qd4, the contingent threat. To obviate this black has two correcting moves, 1 — — Sb5, and 1 — — Se4, each leading to other mates.

The final problem in this chapter, No. 84, features black line openings for white, followed by white self-interference mates. Because of the nature of the material used, however, mates from a pair of pawn batteries form a secondary or incidental theme. The key is 1 Qh7, threatening mate by discovery by the knight's move to g7. The knight cannot mate in the threat line by playing to f4 or to f6 since these moves would cut off the guard from one or the other white pawn in the black king's field. One thematic defense is 1 — — Rc6. This move opens the line of guard for the white rook on a5 to protect the pawn on g5, so that white can play 2 Sf6, shutting off the black rook and also interfering with the bishop on e7, whose guard of the pawn is no longer necessary. The second thematic line is 1 — — PxP ck. This move permits the bishop on d1 to guard the pawn on g4, and so white plays 2 Sf4, interposing on the line of check and also interfering with the rook on c4. Note that the mates in the threat and in the two thematic variations are all given by the knight battery.

SOLUTIONS

NO.69	*1* Rd4	NO.74	*1* Pe4	NO.79	*1* Rf4
NO.70	*1* Rc3	NO.75	*1* Ra6	NO.80	*1* Qf6
NO.71	*1* Qe7	NO.76	*1* Qg8	NO.81	*1* Qd4
NO.72	*1* Qg3	NO.77	*1* KSxP	NO.82	*1* Rb8
NO.73	*1* Ke3	NO.78	*1* QxBP	NO.83	*1* KSd5
		NO.84	*1* Qh7		

9

Schools of Composition

THE CHARACTERISTICS of the work of the composers of The Old School and The Transition School were referred to in Chapter One. In the further development of the chess problem some composers naturally placed the greater emphasis on certain elements, while other composers stressed different elements. In some cases, where a group of composers were closely associated, they often worked toward common standards; in other cases outstanding composers influenced the less experienced and perhaps built up a coterie of disciples. In these ways several distinct schools of composition arose, to which it has been convenient to apply geographical or national names. Editors of problem departments in chess journals, editors of chess columns, problem critics, and tourney judges, all have aided in making the differences between schools more pronounced.

Without going into detail the chief characteristics of the more prominent schools will be described, so the reader will understand references to such schools that he may meet. The schools which will be dealt with briefly are (1) The Old German or Continental School, (2) The English School, (3) The Bohemian School, (4) The American School, and (5) The Modern German School.

Although many eminent composers of other countries displayed the characteristics of The Old German School in their work, that designation is an apt one, since the precepts of the school were advocated for half a century in the German periodical, the *Deutsche Schachzeitung*, founded in 1846. Philipp Klett (*1833–1910*), one of the great leaders of the school, was born in Württemberg, but other distinguished exponents included the Austrians, Dr. Conrad Bayer (*1828–1897*), Dr. Johann N. Berger (*1845-1933*), Konrad Erlin (*1856-1944*), Max Feigl (*1871-1940*), and Ottmar Weiss, known by his pseudonym of Ottmar Nemo, (*1861–1942*); the Rev. J. Jesperson (*1848–1914*) of Denmark, and Emil Pradignat (*1831–1912*) of France. From this national diversity of its adherents it is also called The Continental School.

The followers of this school composed in the "grand Manner," their works being elaborate compositions, combining strategic maneuvering, difficulty of solution and purity of mate in the main lines of play. Dr. Berger, who became the high priest of the school, formulated its ideals in a book published in 1884, entitled *Das Schachproblem, und dessen kunstgerechte Darstellung*. He was so dogmatic that he enunciated his views not as canons of taste but as the rigid laws of a code, which Weenink synopsized as follows:

1. Pure mates are essential in the principal variations.
2. The mates shall be economical, the pieces developing their full activities (for instance, the queen shall not play and mate simply acting as a bishop).
3. White's continuations in the principal lines shall be quiet.
4. No more moves shall be introduced than are required for the expression of the theme.
5. There shall be no short threats; no checking threats; if

need be a threat with quiet moves throughout; but by preference waiting moves.

6. Variations and tries must be introduced; problems containing duals should be reconstructed to embody the dual play as additional variations.

7. White's moves should increase in strength with the progress of the solution, captures and flight-taking moves being avoided in the keys.

8. Problem-schemes born in embryo in the imagination of the composer must be developed and completed according to the problem Laws (*kunstgerecht*).

9. Problems should present a game-like position, ample freedom of attack, and a certain measure of difficulty.

As Weenink comments, the only part of these "Commandments" which has passed "entirely into the discard is the first clause of No. 9. The others are all more or less important still, and are still aimed at by great numbers of composers."

Naturally composers who endeavored to follow such a program felt that compositions of several moves in length were required for the proper development of their ideas, with the result that the school neglected two-movers, omitting them entirely from its composing tournaments. In fact, Klett's ideal problem was the four-mover, but later tendencies made the three-mover more popular. Weenink remarks that "Klett's standard of difficulty was so high, that in many cases his contemporaries failed to solve his problems at all, a result which one may suppose was most gratifying all around!"

The ideals of The English School were considerably different. Composers of this school emphasized variety of play and accuracy of construction, carrying the latter to such an extreme that at times it became a fetish and a handicap in composition. In "The Chess Problem: Text-

Book with Illustrations," or *The Chess Problem Textbook,*
as it is commonly known, which was published in 1886,
Dr. Charles Planck (*1856–1935*) gives the following
Utopian description of his ideal chess problem, for which,
it is interesting to note, he selects, perhaps unconsciously,
four moves as the appropriate length: "Our perfect four-
mover in modern style contains a very quiet but totally
unexpected key-move, threatening mate in the full four-
moves, and leading to eight perfectly distinct and equally
beautiful branches, at least half of which again break up
into three or four different continuations on the penulti-
mate; every mate (and there are upwards of twenty) is
pure, and several also mirrors; the initial position is ele-
gant and natural, captures and checks are conspicuous by
their absence, economy is carried to its utmost limit, every
piece is necessary in every variation; in addition there is
no inaccuracy whatever—not a vestige of a dual to the
apparently most ineffectual defence—no doubled pawns,
no repetition of moves, no short mates; the whole spotless,
perfect, without a blemish. It is needless to point out that
such a position exists only in the composer's wildest
dreams; it is beyond the power of any to produce such a
masterpiece." Although Dr. Planck speaks of this as a wild
dream, the emphasis that he places on variety and on accuracy should be noted.

The characteristics of The English School were exemplified more markedly in the two-move field than in longer
problems, although in the early days of the school more
attention actually was devoted to the three-mover. Among
the leaders in the development of this school were Dr.
Charles Planck, B. G. Laws, who for thirty-three years
was editor of the problem section of the *British Chess
Magazine,* Thomas Tavener (*1856–1928*), P. F. Blake
(*1873–1936*), and Godfrey Heathcote (*1870–1952*). A

little later A. F. Mackenzie, living in Jamaica, exerted great influence.

In the earlier three-move problems of The English School it was considered highly desirable to have the main-play, at least, end in a pure and economical mate, this being regarded as a mark of economical construction. The term "model mate" had not then been coined. Later it became customary to have three-movers and four-movers embody more than one model. The English School, however, never has been so strict as has The Bohemian School in the definition of model mates so far as the use of white pawns is concerned. Accuracy, however, became worshipped to such an extent that in English solving tourneys points were awarded for the noting of any dual continuations or dual mates, even if they were entirely unimportant.

Just as there are changes in the ideals of individual composers, so there are changes in schools, and while the names themselves may persist the standards of a school alter from decade to decade. The tenets of The English School of Laws and Planck, that flourished in the eighteen-nineties and in the earlier years of this century, have been modified in the last three decades. The tendency of recent years has been toward a more balanced treatment of accuracy, as is shown, for example, in the work of Mansfield, who does not attempt to eliminate insignificant duals at the expense of economy. The production of variety for its own sake no longer is sought, a change occasioned primarily by the increasing attention that has been given, throughout the problemistic world, to the study of themes. A highly thematic problem by its very nature may definitely limit the number of mates or of lines of play involved.

České Melodie, the title of the collection of problems

by Josef Pospišil (*1861–1916*), brought out in 1908, had an introduction by B. G. Laws and J. W. Allen, in which they summarized the ideals of The Bohemian School of that period in the following sentences: "The Bohemian composer is pre-occupied with three things mainly. He desires to render two or more variations with a high degree of economical unity; he desires to secure model mates for his principal variations; and he desires to present an attractive initial setting, suggestive of freedom, without over crowding or obviously unnatural arrangements."

The Bohemian School originated in the decade of 1860 to 1870 and Anton König (*1836–1911*) is accredited with being its founder. It soon included such celebrated composers as Dr. Jan Dobruský (*1853–1907*) and Jiři Chocholouš (*1856–1930*), and its tenets were crystallized in the introductory essay, written by Pospišil, to the collection of 321 Bohemian problems which appeared in 1887 under the title *České Úlohy Šachové.*

The true Bohemians regard beauty as the most important element in a problem, and this culminates in the mating positions. Yet Bohemian workmanship is distinguished not merely by the mates themselves but also by the manner in which they are produced. As Weenink states: "it is this very manner of combination, rather than the mates themselves, which constitutes the main principle of the Bohemian standard." Starting with an open and attractive setting, the typical Bohemian composition exhibits great mobility in the movements of the men and considerable variety in method in reaching the model mating positions, which in the later period of The Bohemian School are frequently echoes of each other or are pin-models. Accuracy is not considered an essential in the lines of play that do not lead to the model mates.

Naturally there are many strategic themes that cannot be shown with model mate endings, although Dr. Emil Palkoska (*b. 1871*) has done notable work in showing that many striking themes can be combined with model mates.

The Bohemian School has included a large and illustrious group of composers, the most outstanding of whom by common consent is Miroslav Kostal *(1881–1958)*, or Havel, as he is known to problemists. Similarly to The English School the ideals of The Bohemian School have changed with the years and the compositions of Havel are constructively far different from those of Dobruský and Pospišil. In modern Bohemian composition it has become a *sine qua non* for a problem of tourney standards to have at least three model mates. From the very nature of the problematic elements considered of chief importance by the Bohemians, their compositions are principally three-movers and occasional four-movers. Bohemian principles of construction applied to the two-mover too greatly restrict its possibilities, and so comparatively few Bohemian two-movers are composed.

How far some of the votaries of The Bohemian School carry the principle of economy in composition is indicated by a paragraph in František Dedrle's (*b. 1878*) introduction to *Bohemian Garnets*, the collection of Havel's problems published as the 1923 volume in Alain C. White's *Christmas Series*. Dedrle writes: "Owing to this rigorous adherence to economy the Bohemian school eschews sacrificial combinations and thereby abandons those fireworks which are so dear to the beginner, and which may be regarded as the device of undeveloped art. Sacrifices are in reality a veiled uneconomy, a riddance of superfluous pieces. Therefore we find in Havel's problems very sparing use made of sacrifices, and then only when they form an essential part of the idea."

There has never been an actual American School, in the sense that a school implies a leader with followers or a group of coworkers with common aesthetic standards. The appellation dates from the work of Loyd, who popularized what has been termed the "humorous" element in composition. The utterly unexpected keymove, or possibly a delightfully hidden continuation following a plausible key, leading the solver to believe he is on the wrong trail, have come to be termed Loydesque, because such features were characteristic of so much of his work. Loyd was not greatly concerned with technical polish and beauty of mating positions, but he concentrated his efforts on the illustration of bright ideas, sharply expressed. He did not care for model mates merely as an end in themselves, but he did like a beautiful mate as the termination of a piquant line of play. Any problem of such type was, in the past, labeled as of The American School, and even Dr. Planck, in *The Chess Problem Textbook*, stated: "There are at least three nations whose people have given sufficient attention to the subject to develop a distinct national style in problem composition. The three schools are the Teutonic, the American, and the British. . . . the German excels in depth and beauty, the Englishman in constructive skill, and the American in wit and sharpness of idea."

Although Loyd may not have established a definite school, yet some of the traits of his style greatly influenced other American composers. For example, the high value that many American composers, even of the present generation, place on an unusual keymove or on actual economy in men, are "American" characteristics dating from Loyd.

In many ways the work of William A. Shinkman (*1847–1933*), "The Wizard of Grand Rapids," had similar characteristics to the compositions of Loyd, though Shinkman really developed a style peculiarly his own, notable for the marvellous effects he was able to secure with relatively few men. The majority of Loyd's problems were composed before he came of age in the beginning of the sixties. He had another spurt of composing activity during 1876–1878, and then afterward only brought out an occasional problem. Shinkman, on the other hand began composing about 1870 and continued for over half a century, with an output of some three thousand compositions. With ideals so like those of Loyd, Shinkman had a great influence in the carrying on of the American tradition up to the time of the present generation of composers.

Among the prominent composers of The Old German School were the most famous collaborators in problem history, Johannes Kohtz (*1843–1918*) and Karl Kockelkorn (*1843–1914*), and a collection of their problems was issued in 1875. Years later both became inactive, but about the beginning of the present century Kohtz' interest in composition was again awakened and from a study of the problems of the Transitional Period he was led to change his ideals radically. Discarding the artistic precepts of The Old German School, he proclaimed that the illustration of themes was all important, and this thesis, with the support of a group of younger composers, led to the beginnings of The Modern German School. This school emphasizes what its adherents term the intellectual element in problems, rather than the aesthetic. Composers of this school are concerned with content more than with form. They have made a systematic study of strategic themes, particularly those which involve critical moves.

Today, three-move and longer problems often are

roughly divided into two classes, "strategic" and "model mate" positions, according to whether the composer stresses what might be called kinetic or static effects. As already mentioned, however, Dr. Palkoska has in many instances achieved remarkable success in showing strategic combinations with model mate denouements. The followers of any particular school are not limited either geographically or racially, there being composers in many different parts of the world who pattern their work on Bohemian lines, while others, irrespective of their domicile, are interested only in illustrating strategical themes, with perhaps merely a minor regard for technical polish and with no care at all for model mating positions.

Some composers have developed a style distinctively their own, such as the English composer C. S. Kipping, who specialized in strategic three-movers. Frequently he employed quite unconventional methods of construction, his aim simply being to present sharply some bright strategic idea. A collection of his three-movers was brought out as the 1932 volume of *The Christmas Series*, under the title *The Chessmen Speak*, which is an apt characterization of his style. Then there are certain great composers who experiment with compositions in different styles. An outstanding example is Shinkman's nephew, Otto Wurzburg *(1875–1951)*, who was equally successful in producing both exquisite Bohemian miniatures and highly strategic positions, all his work being distinguished by extreme polish.

Although half a century ago the style of a two-mover may have been affected by the nationality of the composer, especially if he were a disciple of The English or of The Bohemian School, during the last forty years two-move composition as a whole has steadily become more and more internationalized. Accordingly, since the nineties the majority of two-move problems have tended to reflect the standards of composition in general vogue during the particular period in which they were composed. Thus the style of a two-move problem is more apt to indicate the relative date of its composition than to give any clue to the nationality of its composer.

In *A Century of Two-Movers*, published in 1941, Alain White divides the development of modern two-move composition into five principal periods. That from the eighteen-forties to around 1875 saw the two-mover change its general character from a mere puzzle to a work governed by strategic and artistic ideals. The second period, running roughly to the close of the century, covers the discovery of most of the fundamental two-move problematical ideas which differentiate the problem from the played game. The third period, in which tasks were intensively studied, ran to about 1915, when the influence of the Good Companion Club was beginning to be felt. This influence was responsible for the fourth period which continued to 1930, gradually passing into the fifth and present period of two-move composition.

In the earlier days of the two-mover merely an accumulation of variations was often considered a merit in itself, regardless of any thematic relationships. Then the more simple thematic elements, such as flight squares, self-blocks, and interferences, began to be exploited. Unpinning of white by black was the next upward step in the strategic scale, and around the beginning of the century came the cross-checks, popularized largely by Mackenizie's great series of prize winning problems. The maximum defensive powers of individual black pieces were studied, and the task problem became a vogue. The task problem of the first decade of the century, however, was generally limited to a single simple theme and did not involve a combination of themes. Problems 1, 2, 8, and 17 were composed during this period and are typical of it.

The Good Companion movement came almost as an era of renaissance for the two-mover. It may be looked upon as the time when the combination, or blending, of themes began to become dominant in two-movers, and soon composers were using the term "theme complex." Undoubtedly one great factor in this development was the intensive study of the half-pin that dated from 1915. The half-pin lends itself with remarkable ease to combination with other strategic elements, as self-blocks, interferences, unpins, line openings, and cross-checks. Consequently such combinations appeared in more and more protean blendings, resulting in the complex two-mover so typical of the Good Companion period.

Styles in problem composition do not remain stationary. The Good Companions disbanded after ten years and gradual changes both in the subject matter and in the constructive form of two-movers became noticeable. Although Mansfield had been exceedingly active as a Good Companion, his problems usually showed a more restrained style than that of many Good Companion compositions, since he did not strain so much for ultimate task effects or for bewildering complications. During the nineteen-twenties the tendency of other leading two-move composers also was to veer from extreme complications toward more artistic settings of themes. The work of the brilliant Schiffmann is typical of the latter part of this period; his problems exhibiting a more simple style and more open settings than the complicated positions of the Good Companion days.

Alain White points out that while prior to 1915 "progress in the composition of two-movers had rested in great measure in the hands of American and English problemists," since then outstanding two-move composers have appeared in all parts of the world. Especially notable has been a group of Russians, including M. M. Barulin (*d. 194–*), L. A. Issaiev (*d. 1932*) and S. S. Lewman (*d. 194–*), who have given especial attention to the study of compensating play, particularly as exemplified in simultaneous line openings and closings.

Whereas during the first thirty years of this century most of the emphasis in two-movers was placed on the interplay of the black men, the period dating roughly from 1930 may be broadly described as one in which relatively greater attention is being given to the interplay of the white men. The period therefore is characterized more by a change in matter than by one in constructive technique. The two-move composer, who is composing in today's mode, is chiefly occupied with illustrating dual avoidance and contingent threats, both largely involving "white" elements, and also with line openings and line closings, especially as they affect the white pieces. In such problems the line openings and closings usually are of a compensating character; the shutting off of one line of white guard being compensated by the opening of another line. Furthermore, in these problems it is customary to illustrate the theme by at least two echoing or contrasting lines of play.

Problem 84, shown in the last chapter, illustrates compensating white line openings and closings in its two thematic variations. Another problem which exemplifies, in the modern mode, the cutting off of unessential white guards is No. 5 in Chapter Two.

10

Types of Three and Four Move Problems

BESIDES considering problems as examples of different schools of composition or as preeminently either model mate or strategic compositions, they may be grouped according to the forces employed, or classified by various types of settings or by the character of the play. Some of these points will be discussed in this chapter in connection with the illustrative problems, which incidentally are all "model mate" compositions.

In 1898–99 the *New York Sun* held a tourney in which the three-movers were divided according to the forces employed into "Lightweights," "Middleweights," and "Heavyweights," like classifications for pugilists. Nowadays, however, the only distinctive type of three-move or longer problem based on the total number of men, is the *miniature,* which has a maximum limit of seven men. The term is rarely applied to two-movers, whereas Meredith, defined in Chapter Three, is commonly used only in connection with two-movers. Many composing contests have been held exclusively for miniatures and, despite the frequency of anticipations in so restricted a field, these tourneys occasionally yield some novel and beautiful com-

85

First Prize
Four-Move Section
Second Cheney Miniature
Tourney
Cincinnati Enquirer
May 10, 1936

White mates in four moves

86

American Chess Bulletin
February, 1927

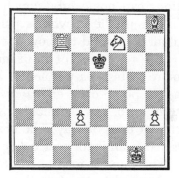

White mates in four moves

87

American Chess Bulletin
November, 1924

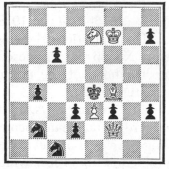

White mates in three moves

88

The Pittsburgh Post
July 11, 1926

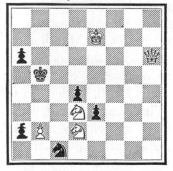

White mates in four moves

positions. Nos. 85 and 86 are examples of miniatures.

Sometimes a composer experiments by restricting himself to the use of only certain men, such as the limitation of the white forces to king, rooks and pawns; Chapter Sixteen being devoted to an examination of problems of this particular type. Where the black force is limited to the king, the problem is a *lone king* problem. Such positions can not exhibit much strategy and whatever they have must lie in white's play. Problem 86 is a lone king affair composed to show the echo of a model mate.

The repetition of the same type of position in two or more mates of a problem is known as an *echo*. Ordinarily a composer only endeavors to echo model mates. The term echo, less commonly, is also applied to two or more similar lines of play. The next chapter is devoted to a detailed examination of echoes of model mates.

The interest in problem 86 lies in the character of the mates and in the fact that there are no checking moves prior to the mates, in other words the continuations are "quiet." It happens that the particular model mate echoed in No. 86 was shown in 1877 by Samuel Loyd, and by the Swiss composer, Paul Johner (*1888–1938*), in 1904. By employing a five-move setting the echo can be quadrupled, as was shown by W. Pauly (*1876–1934*) in 1918, and by Dr. A. Mandler in 1922. These positions showing the echo of this model mate before No. 86 was composed, are mentioned to illustrate the likelihood of the occurrence of anticipations in the miniature field.

Three- and four-movers may have striking keys, as in No. 87 and No. 88, and such keys are by no means incompatible with continuations leading to several model mates as the reader will note. In a problem with so few white pieces as No. 87 a sacrificial key is unexpected, especially since it also yields two flight squares. The key of No. 88,

89

Second Honorable Mention
Informal Tourney
July–December, 1933
The Western Morning News
and Daily Gazette

White mates in three moves

90

The Observer
September 25, 1926

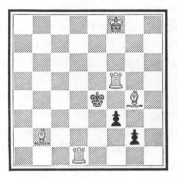

White mates in three moves

91

The Western Morning News
and Mercury
March 27, 1926

White mates in three moves

92

Commended
Eleventh Informal Tourney
The Weekly Westminster
August 9, 1924

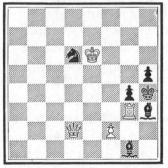

White mates in three moves

at first glance, would seem to place the white queen even further out of play than she is in the initial position. Although such features may be very pleasing, they are not a basis for any kind of problem classification, since ordinarily they are not related to the theme of the problem.

Waiting move three- and four-movers are much less common than in the case of two-movers, and in solving a three- or four-mover the solver usually expects a threat key. Hence a waiting move position, such as No. 89, may prove relatively difficult to solve. Occasionally a composer will construct a position expressly designed to deceive the solver, although when this is the raison d'etre of the problem, it must be looked upon more as a humorous trick than as a legitimate chess problem.

Problem No. 90 was published originally because of the try 1 Rf7. The position shows a model mate echo in an economical setting, but the echo is such a familiar one that whatever claim for novelty the position may have lies in black's defense to 1 Rf7. The white king is placed at f8 to limit the number of squares to which the king's rook can play and so to add to the impression that perhaps the key really is 1 Rf7.

The next problem, No. 91, was composed primarily to show the pin-model mates 1 Qh8, Kd4; 2 SxR ck, Ke5; 3 Pf4, and 1 —— PxS; 2 QxQ ck, Re5; 3 SxKP. A *pin-model mate* is similar to other model mates except that there is also involved a long-range white piece that pins a black man, which if not pinned could prevent the mate. The use of this white piece is not uneconomical because its presence is essential to the mate. If the pinned black man happens to stand in the king's field so that it blocks a square, the fact that the pinning white piece also guards that square is not considered as affecting the character of the model mate. In the first variation of No. 91, for example, the pinned black queen is in the king's field when mate occurs. In the second variation, on the other hand, the pinned rook is not in the king's field. Both mates are regarded as models.

Returning, after this digression on pin-models, to the subject of difficulty resulting from tries, problem 91 is an example of a position where tries occur incidentally. After the problem was composed the author found that, as a mere happenstance, there were such tries. One of them, 1 Qa8, has proved deceptive to many solvers, since it can be defeated only by one rather obscure defense. Probably numerous solvers, however, have found the correct key without even noticing this try.

This position also illustrates what has been variously termed a "lazy" or "slaughter" model mate. To produce such a mate black has to capture a white piece not required in the mate, the capture not being forced nor even a purposively defensive move, but a merely aimless one. Thus in No. 91 the threat is 2 Sd3; 3 Bb2. This threat follows 1 — — QxQ, and then if black obligingly captures the knight on d6 by 2 — — PxS or 2 — — RxS, the ensuing mate becomes a model. Such a mate might well be called a "cooperative model," since black must cooperate with white to produce it. A model of this character is obviously artificial and has little aesthetic value.

Although Bohemian purists may frown on sacrifices that are employed merely to produce model mating positions, sacrificial play may be made the theme of a problem, such as No. 92, in which the rook is sacrificed on the second move in three different lines of play. In the next position there are three sacrifices of the queen leading to model mates, with a fourth model occurring after the defense 1 — — Rd8 ck. Note that in the case of each of these sacrifices black is obliged to remove the white queen by capturing her.

The model mates in No. 93 all take place in the center of the board, where the black king's field comprises nine squares. The term center-of-board model is seldom seen, but *side-of-board model* is in common use, being applied to cases where the black king stands on a square at the edge of the board when mated. Five such side-of-board models are found in problem 94. Side-of-board models are usually easier to construct than are other models, because there are three less squares in the king's field to be controlled. On this account models away from the edge of the board, where the black king has nine squares in his field, are commonly regarded as of a higher value. When the king is in a corner of the board only four squares have to be controlled in arranging model mates, but the mating positions in themselves have much less possibilities for variety, and so generally in *king-in-the-corner* problems the chief interest has to lie in the play leading to the mates. No. 99 is an exception to this rule, since it is a problem in which the interest lies in the character of the mating positions.

In problem No. 94 all but one of the second-move continuations are quiet moves. This is considered a meritorious quality, since such moves please the solver because they seem less aggressive than checking moves.

Many problems are composed of the general character of No. 95, which combines some degree of strategic play with model mating positions. In this composition the strategic feature is the ambushing of the white queen behind two other men. The problem, however, does not illustrate any outstanding theme and the models are commonplace.

93

*Commended
Informal Tourney
July–December, 1935
The Western Morning News
and Daily Gazette*

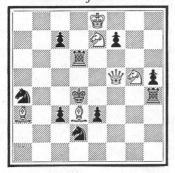

White mates in three moves

94

*Prager Presse
May 1, 1926*

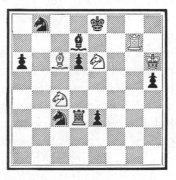

White mates in three moves

95

*First Prize
Informal Tourney
January–June, 1925
The Western Morning News
and Mercury*

White mates in three moves

96

*The Observer
February 28, 1926*

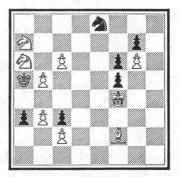

White mates in three moves

Mechanical types of model mate problems may be constructed in which black's moves have no strategic defensive value and such problems may degenerate into a mere assemblage of model mating positions. Despite superficial resemblances these are not true Bohemian problems, because in the latter variety of play and considerable mobility in the men employed are also essential elements. No. 96, with its five technically different models mates, narrowly approaches this mechanical type of composition. It possibly is redeemed by the fact that the two black knight moves, which produce the variations, actually defend against the threat. Furthermore, the threat line in itself is a little out of the usual. Brian Harley, editor of *The Observer* chess column, commented: "The key is the first a player of the game would choose, a rare thing in a problem, but the P is never actually queened, preferring the lesser honor of knighthood; the way in which the P on R6, used also as a block, forces this selection, is admirable."

A common mechanical form of model mate problem results from the use of a *mating net*, which Weenink describes as follows: "The mating net, or process of alternating the white moves, is equivalent to placing all the white officers in a mating position and then seeing on how many squares the black king can stand checkmated. The problem will then be reconstructed backward, by providing a solution in the course of which the white forces reach the mating position through an alternation of moves." In a problem of this kind the black king usually has two or more flight squares.

Mating net construction is illustrated in problem 97, in which black's moves have practically no defensive value, the king playing to one square or another indifferently. The position is saved from seeming too mechanical by the mobility of the four white pieces, every one of which has to move in each line of play of the solution. The key gives the black king an additional flight square and because of this and of the character of the mating positions, the problem appealed to the tourney judge, B. G. Laws.

No. 98 is practically a task composition, the three thematic mates all being given by the queen's pawn. Although the mating positions are not echoes of each other the fact that the pawn is always the mating man gives the problem a high degree of constructive unity. The mate in the threat line is not a model unless black cooperates by removing one of the knights by capture, i. e., 1 Qc2, PxS; 2 Be4 ck (threat), QxB; 3 PxQ. 1 —— QxB; 2 Qa2 ck, Kc5; 3 Pd4. (This mate is not a model since the square c4 is doubly guarded.) 1 —— Sc5; 2 Qc4 ck, PxQ; 3 PxP. In the first and third lines the play leads to what are termed *return capture mates.*

Pin-models were shown in two variations of problem 91, and there also is one in No. 95, viz., 1 Qb1, Bb2; 2 Qb4, threat 3 Sf3. Problem 99 has pin-models in all three of its thematic lines. 1 Qb7, BxR; 2 Qh1 ck, Bb1; 2 Sc2. 1 —— Ph2; 2 Qh1, QxB; 3 RxR. 1 —— Qc3; 2 RxR ck, BxR; 3 Sc2.

Problem 100 is introduced to illustrate several points. It was specifically composed to show model mates in which a relatively large number of white pieces participate in each mate. It has three models, and four white pieces, exclusive of the king, take part in each of these mates, a fifth white piece being sacrificed during the play in each variation. At one time it was considered highly desirable to have the mates in a model mate problem diverse in character, and those in this composition include a lateral mate by the rook, a diagonal mate by the queen, and a knight mate in a mirror setting. Such variety of mates naturally is far more attractive than several mates of a similar type without any distinguishing features to make them individually interesting. If the similar mates, however, are echoes of each other this fact in itself creates interest and often there is a pleasurable element of surprise to the solver in finding one mate to be the echo of another.

There are two other points that No. 100 illustrates. First, the white pawn in this problem takes part in only one of the three model mates. This would be condoned, or even pass unnoticed, by followers of the English School, but would be deprecated by Bohemian artists. Its presence shows that the author did not have the requisite constructive skill to arrange a model mating position without having to employ the pawn to guard f6.

Then, as mentioned heretofore, extreme purists of the Bohemian School do not look with favor on the sacrificing of white men in order to produce model mates, holding that if it is necessary to get a man out of the way through a sacrifice, the presence of that man in the initial position of the problem is really a breach of economy. This, however, is a technical refinement that few composers heed. Such a tenet is a far cry from the standards of the earlier days of composing, when sacrifices were the most prominent element in problem composition, doubtless because composition had not then moved so far away from over-the-board play, in which sacrifices are always regarded as brilliancies.

All the problems shown in this chapter would be acceptable as model mate compositions to the English School, but only Nos. 85, 87, 88, 90, 92, 93, 94, 97 and 98 meet the strictest Bohemian requirements, and Bohemian purists might even look askance at the sacrificial features

97

Second Prize
Four-Move Section
Thirteenth Informal Tourney
The Westminster Gazette
April 21, 1926

White mates in four moves

98

Second Honorable Mention
Informal Tourney
January–June, 1934
The Western Morning News
and Daily Gazette

White mates in three moves

99

V. The Western Morning
News and Daily Gazette
May 22, 1937

White mates in three moves

100

British Chess Magazine
January, 1925

White mates in three moves

of No. 88 and also possibly regard No. 97 as too much of the mating net type.

SOLUTIONS

NO.85
1 Se3, *threat* 2 Sf5 ck, Kh5; 3 Ph4, any;   4 Rg5
　　　　Kh5; 2 Sg2, B any; 3 Sf4 ck, Kh4; 4 Rg4
　　　　　　　　　　　　　　　　　　Kh6; 4 Rg6
　　　Bd5; 2 SxB, Kh5;   3 Sf4 ck, *etc.*

NO.86
1 Rb7, Kd5; 2 Sd8, Kc5; 3 Be5, Kd5; 4 Rb5
　　　　　　　　　　Kd6; 3 Bd4, Kd5; 4 Rd7
　　Kf5; 2 Rb6, Kf4; 3 Kf2, Kf5; 4 Rf6

NO.87
1 Sf5, *threat* 2 Sd6 ck, Kd5; 3 Pe4
　　　Kd5; 2 Sd6, Kc5;   3 Pe4
　　　Sc4; 2 Sg3 ck, Kd5; 3 Pe4
　　　KxS; 2 QxBP, any;   3 Pe4

NO.88
1 Qh1, SxS; 2 Qb7 ck, Kc5; 3 Se4 ck, Kc4; 4 Pb3
　　　　　　　　　　　Ka5; 3 Sc4 ck, Ka4; 4 Pb3
　　　　　　　　　　　Ka4; 3 Pb3 ck, Ka3; 4 Sc4
　　　PxS; 2 Qb7 ck, Kc4; 3 Se5 ck, Kc5; 4 Pb4
　　　Kb6; 2 Sc4 ck, Kb5; 3 Qd5 ck, Ka4; 4 Sb6

NO.89
1 Kg7, Pa4;　　　　2 Qb4 ck, KxP; 3 Pd4
　　　　Pb5;　　　　2 Pe3 ck, Kc4; 3 Pd3
　　　Kc4, KS any; 2 Qa4 ck, Kc5; 3 Pd4

NO.90
1 Rf6, Ke3; 2 Bd4 ck, K any; 3 BxP
  Pg1=Q; 2 BxP ck, Ke3;   3 Bd4
  Pg1=S; 2 Bc1, etc.

NO.91
1 Qh8, Kd4; 2 SxR ck, Ke5;   3 Pf4
        PxS; 2 QxQ ck, Re5;   3 SxP
        QxQ; 2 Sd3 (*threat*), RxS; 3 Bb2

NO.92
1 Qe3, BxP; 2 RxB ck (*threat*), PxR; 3 Qf4
      Bh2; 2 KxS, BxR ck;   3 PxB
      Bg2, f1; 2 RxP ck, KxR;   3 Qg3
                  PxR;   3 Qh6

NO.93
1 Be2, *threat* 2 Qd5 ck, RxQ; 3 Sc6
        Pc2; 2 Qc5 ck, SxQ; 3 Bb2
        Re4; 2 QxR ck, SxQ; 3 Sf3
        Rd8 ck; 2 KxR, Pc2; 3 Qf6

NO.94
1 Sb6, *threat* 2 SxB, SxS;   3 BxS
        SxB; 2 Sc7 ck, Kd8; 3 RxB
                  Kf8; 3 SxB
        BxB; 2 Sc8, *threat*   3 Re7
        Se4; 2 Sa8, BxB;   3 QSc7
        Sd5; 2 Sc8, *etc.*

NO.95
1 Qb1, Bc2, c6 *or* Pd5; 2 Qb4, *threat*   3 Sf3
                          KxP; 3 Qe7
                  Sg3; 2 QxP ck, SxQ; 3 Sf3
                          KxP; 3 Qe7
            KxP; 2 Qb6, *threat*   3 Qd8

NO.96
1 Pc7, Pa2; 2 Pc8=S, any; 3 Bb6
    SxP; 2 SxS, any;   3 Sc6
    Sd6; 2 Sb8, SxP;   3 Sa7—c6
            else; 3 Sb8—c6

NO.97
1 Sa5, Pc1=Q; 2 Sa6 ck, Kb6;   3 BxPc7 ck, any; 4 Bc4
                        Kb5;   3 Bc4 ck, any;   4 BxPc7
        Kb6; 2 Sb8—c6, Pc1=Q; 3 Bd4 ck, Kb5;   4 Bc4
        Kb5; 2 Sb8—c6, Pc1=Q; 3 Bc4 ck, Kc5;   4 Bd4

NO.98
1 Qc2, PxS; 2 Be4 ck (threat), QxB; 3 PxQ
    QxB; 2 Qa2 ck, Kc5;   3 Pd4
    Sc5; 2 Qc4 ck, PxQ;   3 PxP

NO.99
1 Qb7, BxR; 2 Qh1 ck, Bb1; 3 Sc2
    Ph2; 2 Qh1, QxB;   3 RxR
    Qc3; 2 RxR ck, BxR; 3 Sc2

NO.100
1 Sc4, KxS; 2 Rd6 (threat), Kb4; 3 Rd4
    KxR; 2 Qf4, Kd5;   3 Qf7
    Pe3; 2 Qh1 ck, KxR;   3 Sd4

11

Model Mate Echoes

THE REPETITION, or echoing, of a mating position in two or more lines of play may be regarded as constituting the theme of a problem. Various examples of such echoes are given in this chapter to show a few of the mates that appear more or less commonly in such compositions.

In 1927 Alain White included in his *Christmas Series* a volume by František Dedrle, entitled *Echo*, in which 355 different forms of model mate echoes are shown, with one or more actual problems illustrating each form of echo.

Where the black king stands on squares of the same color in each of the echoed mates it is a *monochrome echo*. Where the king stands on a white square in one mate and on a black square in another it is a *chameleon echo*.

The examples given in this chapter are arranged according to the following classification:

MONOCHROME ECHOES

CHAMELEON ECHOES

In problem 101 there are three mates which are of such a character that they may be considered as echoes. In each of the three the black king stands on a black square so that the mates are monochrome echoes. The play is as follows: 1 Ba6, Kc5; 2 Qb5 ck, Kd4; 3 Qe5. This is a pin-model and the white rook takes an actual part in the mate, since by pinning the pawn it nullifies the pawn's guard on e5. 1 — — Kd5; 2 Qd3 ck, Kc5; 3 QxP. 1 — — Kc7; 2 Qb7 ck, KxR; 3 Qe7. If there were a ninth rank of squares this mate would be seen to be like the preceding two, the supported queen attacking six squares in the black king's field with the bishop guarding two white squares diagonally. The problem also has a fourth model that is not an echo: 1 — — RxR; 2 Qb5 ck, Kc7; 3 Qb7.

101

Commended
Eleventh Informal Tourney
The Weekly Westminster
August 23, 1924

102

Prager Presse
July 25, 1926

White mates in three moves

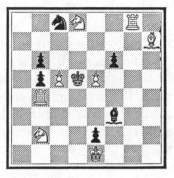

White mates in three moves

103

First Commended
Informal Tourney
January–June, 1937
The Western Morning News
and Daily Gazette

104

Chemnitzer Tageblatt und
Anzeiger
February 13, 1927

White mates in three moves

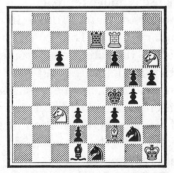

White mates in three moves

The next problem, No. 102, not only has echoed rook mates, but echoed play leading to the mating positions. The black king stands on the same square in each of the echoed mates, the echo resulting from the fact that the mates are delivered by different rooks, on different sides of the black king. The position has two constructive weaknesses. First, the key rook moves from an outlying square to an aggressive location, although it does offer itself as a sacrifice. Second, white's king's knight does not move but throughout all the lines of play it acts simply as a guard. If a white piece serves merely as a guard in one variation, it is desirable to have it take an active role in another. The white pawns take an active part in all the principal lines, one remaining as a guard in each of the three model mates.

No. 103 is another problem which meets the standards of the English School but not those of the Bohemian, the followers of which would object to white's queen's bishop's pawn because it takes part in but one of the four model mates in the composition. The white pawn on f4 is captured by black in three of the lines leading to model mating positions and gives the mate in the fourth line. So its use is above reproach. The pawn on c4, however, serves merely to guard a square in one model mate and in a secondary mate. This composition has two mates by the bishop that are monochrome echoes, and it also has two other model mates. In two of the mates the white men are on exactly the same squares, while the black king is on different squares. These count as distinct mates, because of the change in position of the king. The order of moves leading to the mates is different and mate is given by different pieces.

Problem 104 has two monochrome echoes of a rather unusual type, and a third model that is not an echo. In

105

*American Chess Bulletin
March–April, 1944*

White mates in three moves

106

*Honor Problem
Chess Review
May, 1936*

White mates in three moves

107

*The Westminster Gazette
July 26, 1926*

White mates in four moves

108

*Chess Review
August, 1937*

White mates in three moves

order to secure the echo, however, the author used all the black pawns in the set, so that although the composition may be technically correct, it is an unattractive affair. The echo is 1 Kh2, Ph4; 2 RxP ck, Ke5; 3 SxP, and 1 — — Ke5; 2 RxR ck, Kd6; 3 Sf5.

Chameleon echoes, as a rule, are both more difficult to construct and of greater interest to the solver than are monochrome echoes, particularly when the mates are of a complex character or when some unexpected lines of play are required to produce them. In the case of many forms of chameleon echoes at least four moves are necessary to maneuver the men into the mating positions. All the remaining problems in this chapter show chameleon echoes. In the problems used as illustrations in the preceding chapter, No. 86 shows monochrome echoes, while examples of chameleon echoes appear in Nos. 85, 90 and 97.

The threat line in No. 105 leads to a model mate of which there is a chameleon echo when black defends by 1 — — Pg6. The white pawns, unfortunately, are required for a mate after 1 — — Ph5. In No. 106 there are echoed chameleon models, with the queen functioning as a rook in one of the mates. Both of the echoed mates in this problem occur in the threat line of play, which is not so desirable as having them in separate lines. 1 Rf1, threat 2 Sb4 ck, Kc4; 3 Rc1, or 2 — — Ke5; 3 Qe8. It will be noted that there are slight differences between the manner in which the queen guards the queen's knight in the first mate and that in which the rook guards the king's knight in the second, but these dissimilarities merely make the general effect of the two mates more attractive. Echoes that are exact in every detail sometimes seem too mechanical.

Problem 107 shows echoed chameleon side-of-board models, and a four-move setting is required to permit the knight to guard the necessary squares. The black king, in three lines of play, is mated on h6, h5 and h4 in turn by the rook. The first two of these are echoed models. The third mate is not a model because g3 is doubly guarded.

Problem 108 has three mates that are sufficiently similar to be considered echoes, since in each the mate is delivered by a bishop supported by the knight, with the other two white pieces acting as guards. Yet each of these mates differs from the others in some minor respect that enhances rather than detracts from its interest. 1 Qb1, Kc7; 2 Bf4 ck (threat), Kb7; 2 Bc8. 1 — — Pc5; 2 Bf4 ck, Kc6; 3 Bd5. These two mates have a resemblance to the echoed mates in problem 103, except that in that problem the queen guards the knight diagonally, while here the guard is along the file. Finally, 1 — — Ke5; 2 Sc4 ck, Kd4; 3 Be3, is a chameleon echo of the other two models.

Constructively No. 109 may remind the reader of No. 104 because of the large number of black men employed to prevent any possible escape of the black king, who is smothered by his friends. The echo here is too mechanical to be as pleasing as those in some of the other problems, and the position is reproduced only because the models are of an uncommon type.

In No. 110 the actual mates are similar to those in problem 104. In No. 104, however, the king in the two echoed mates stands on black squares which are diagonally adjacent, while the echoed mates in No. 110 are given on laterally adjacent squares. In order to give the knight time to get into position to deliver these mates a four-move setting is needed. The mating position in this problem, with knight, rook and a single bishop, is a familiar one and the originality of the problem lies solely in the development of the echo. The pawns in this posi-

tion are an unavoidable constructive evil. The echo runs:
1 Bg5, Ke5; 2 Rd8, KxB; 3 Rd5 ck, Ke6; 4 Sf4, or
3 — — Ke4; 4 Sf6. This in itself is a monochrome echo.
1 — — Kd4 or Kd6; 2 Sf6, Ke5; 3 Rc5 ck, Kd6; 4 Se4,
results in a chameleon echo of the preceding mates, the
queen's bishop having a role in the mate since it guards e7.

The use of a white pawn, initially standing on its home
square, to produce two echoing lines of play or two
echoed mates, has been termed by the author *pawn-one-
two play*. In 1935–1936 he held a tourney in the *American
Chess Bulletin* for problems based on this feature and
over fifty entries were received. The white pawn when
standing on its home square is peculiarly adapted to give
chameleon echoed mates because of its option of moving
either one or two squares, and the remaining problems
in this chapter show such chameleon mates by pawns
supported by different white pieces.

In Nos. 111 and 112 the pawn is supported by the king.
In the former the mechanics of the play is exceedingly
simple and whatever charm the problem may have comes
from this very simplicity. No. 112, on the other hand, has
lines of some strategical interest, produced by the defensive play of the black bishop and knight.

In the next three compositions the mating pawn is
supported by the white queen, vertically in No. 113 and
diagonally in No. 114 and No. 115. Besides being an illustration of chameleon echoed pawn mates, No. 114 is
also a good example of mobility of the white men, a
feature which was mentioned in Chapter Ten in connection with problem 97, although other problems such as
No. 93 and No. 94 show mobility to an equal extent. In
No. 114 the black king, standing first on the fifth rank
and then on the fourth, is mated by the bishop's pawn
supported by the queen; the queen's pawn, supported by

109

The Pittsburgh Post
July 4, 1926

White mates in four moves

110

First Honorable Mention
Four-Move Section
First Tourney of National
Chess Federation of U. S. A.
1928

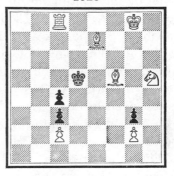

White mates in four moves

111

First Prize
Three-Move Section
Second Cheney Miniature
Tourney
Cincinnati Enquirer
May 10, 1936

White mates in three moves

112

American Chess Bulletin
January, 1936

White mates in four moves

the rook, guarding two squares in the king's field. In the first line of play all four of these white men move from their initial positions, and in the second line all move except the queen's pawn. A four-mover, somewhat similar in setting, in which the support of the guarding pawn was given by the white king instead of by the rook, was composed by P. K. Traxler (*1866–1936*) a quarter of a century previously (Appendix A9). The author found the support of the guarding pawn by the rook difficult to work out and this problem is one of his personal favorites. In addition to the primary lines of play with the echoed model mates given by the pawn, there are also secondary lines with echoed rook mates, one of which, however, is not a model.

When the pawn in No. 115, supported diagonally by the queen, delivers the chameleon echoed model mates, the knight guards two squares in the king's field. The constructional difficulty of arranging these knight guards was considerable, and the aggressive keymove was occasioned by the impossibility of avoiding cooks if the knight were placed nearer the black king in the initial setting. In addition to the echoed pawn models, this problem also has a second set of echoes which are not models. The solution runs: 1 Sd2, Ph6; 2 Se4 (threat), Pd6; 3 Sf2 ck, Kh4; 4 Pg3, or 1 — — Pd6; 2 Qe6 ck, Kh5; 3 Sf3, threat 4 Pg4. The echoes that are not models are: 1 — — Ph6; 2 Se4, Pg5; Sf6 ck, Kh4; 4 Qh2, and 1 — — Pd6; 2 Qe6 ck, Kh5; 3 Sf3, Pg6; 4 Qh3. In each of these mates black's knight's pawn forms a self-block, as it advances one or two squares, thus making interesting secondary lines in a problem where the play in the primary lines features the play of white's knight's pawn.

Probably the easiest method of constructing a problem with echoing model mates given by a pawn is to have the

113

Commended
Thirteenth Informal Tourney
The Westminster Gazette
July 10, 1926

White mates in four moves

114

First Honorable Mention
Four-Move Section
Fourteenth Informal Tourney
The Westminster Gazette
February 26, 1927

White mates in four moves

115

American Chess Bulletin
February, 1936

White mates in four moves

116

British Chess Magazine
November, 1937

White mates in three moves

pawn supported by a rook above it on the same file, since the rook also acts as a guard for all the squares on the file above the pawn. This arrangement is shown in problem 116. In No. 117 the echoed mates are given by different pawns, each being supported in turn by the rook from above.

Instead of having the pawn supported by a rook from above it is a more difficult task for the composer to arrange the support from below, as in No. 118, which is the author's favorite lightweight among his three-movers.

Problem 119 shows chameleon echoed model mates given by two alternating pawns supported by the bishops, with a third model following 1 — — Kb4, etc. Finally, No. 120 illustrates echoed pin-models by a pawn, the drawback to this problem from a constructional point of view being that, in order for the mates to be models, black must first capture the white bishop with knight or pawn.

In Chapter Sixteen, problem 186 shows chameleon echoed model mates delivered by a pawn supported laterally by a rook. Then in No. 187 there are chameleon echoed model mates by a pawn, supported by a rook vertically, that follow echoed lines of play, each of which involves a rook sacrifice to provide a clearance for the pawn and also to induce a black self-block.

While for any type of problem an economical setting is desirable, it is particularly so in echoed model mate compositions. Here the chief element of interest is the beauty of the mating positions, and the solver's pleasure increases proportionately to the economy by which the mates are produced. Another feature of importance in this kind of problem is the attractiveness of the initial position. In strategic compositions these features do not rate so high relatively, although always desirable.

117

*First Honorable Mention
Three-Move Section
First Tourney of National
Chess Federation of U. S. A.
1928*

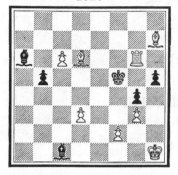

White mates in three moves

118

*Second and Third
Honorable Mention (ex aequo)
Informal Tourney
January–June, 1936
The Western Morning News*

White mates in three moves

119

*V. British Chess Magazine
September, 1926*

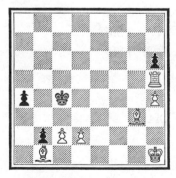

White mates in four moves

120

*Second and Third
Honorable Mention (ex aequo)
Informal Tourney
January–June, 1936
The Western Morning News*

White mates in three moves

SOLUTIONS

(Only the lines ending in model mates are given)

NO.101

1 Ba6, Kc5; 2 Qb5 ck, Kd4; 3 Qe5
         Kd5; 2 Qd3 ck, Kc5; 3 QxP
         Kc7; 2 Qb7 ck, KxR; 3 Qe7
         RxR; 2 Qb5 ck, Kc7; 3 Qb7

NO.102

1 KRg4, SPxP; 2 KRd4 ck, PxR; 3 RxSP
        BPxP; 2 QRd4 ck, PxR; 3 Rg5
         BxR; 2 Be4 ck, KxKP; 3 Sd3

NO.103

1 Bh4, *threat* 2 Qh7 ck, KxP; 3 BxP
          BxP; 2 Qh7 ck, Ke5; 3 Bf6
          KxP; 2 BxP ck, Kf5; 3 Qh7
          Pe5; 2 SxP ck, Kg6; 3 Pf5

NO.104

1 Kh2, Ph4; 2 RxP ck, Ke5;   3 SxP
        Ke5; 2 RxR ck, Kd6;   3 Sf5
        RxR; 2 Bg3 ck (*threat*), Ke3; 3 Sf5

NO.105

1 Ra6, Pa3; 2 Ra5 ck, Kg6; 3 Qf5
        Pg6; 2 RxPa4, Ph5; 3 Qf4

NO.106

1 Rf1, *threat* 2 Sb4 ck, Kc4; 3 Rc1
                         Ke5; 3 Qe8

NO.107
1 Sg4, Kh5; 2 Sf6 ck, Kh6; 3 Pf5, any; 4 Rg6
Pd2; 2 Sh6, Kh5;   3 Sf5, any; 4 Rg5

NO.108
1 Qb1, Kc7; 2 Bf4 ck (*threat*), Kb7; 3 Bc8
Pc5; 2 Bf4 ck, Kc6;   3 Bd5
Ke5; 2 Sc4 ck, Kd4;   3 Be3

NO.109
1 Se5, Kd5; 2 Be8, Kc5;   3 Bd6 ck, Kd5; 4 Bc6
                threat 3 Bc6 ck, Kc5; 4 Bd6
Ke3; 2 QBxP ck, Ke4; 3 BxP ck, KxS; 4 Bd4

NO.110
1 Bg5, Ke5; 2 Rd8, KxB; 3 Rd5 ck, Ke6; 4 Sf4
                                Ke4; 4 Sf6
Kd4, d6; 2 Sf6, Ke5;   3 Rc5 ck, Kd6; 4 Se4

NO.111
1 Pe4, Pe5; 2 Qf5 ck, Kh4; 3 Pg3
Kh5; 2 Kf3, Pe5;   3 Pg4

NO.112
1 Kd2, Pd5; 2 Kc2, Bd7; 3 Qc5, *threat*   4 Pb3
Sd8; 2 Kc3, Sc6; 3 QxS ck, Ka5; 4 Pb4

NO.113
1 Sf6, PxP; 2 Qb7, Kc5;   3 SxP ck, Kc4; 4 Pb3
Kc5; 2 Sd7 ck, Kc6; 3 Se5 ck, Kc5; 4 Pb4
Pf4; 2 Sd7, Pf3 ck; 3 Kd2, Pf2;   4 Pb3

NO.114
1 Qa6, Kd4; 2 QxPa5, Pf3;   3 RxP, P moves; 4 Pc3
PxP; 2 Rf4, P moves; 3 Pd4, P moves; 4 Pc4
Ke5; 3 Qf6 ck, *etc.*
Pf3; 2 Pc3, any;   3 Rb2, any;   4 Rb5

NO.115

1 Sd2, Ph6; 2 Se4 (*threat*), Pd6; 3 Sf2 ck, Kh4; 4 Pg3
                                    Pg5; 3 Sf6 ck, *etc.*

       Pd6; 2 Qe6 ck, Kh5;   3 Sf3, *threat*   4 Pg4
                                              Pg6; 4 Qh3

NO.116

1 QRg6, *threat* 2 Rg5 ck, Kh4; 3 Pg3
             Rf2; 2 QxR, any;   3 Pg4

NO.117

1 Bc7, *threat* 2 Rd6 ck, Ke5; 3 Pd4
         Ph4; 2 Pf3, PxBP;   3 Pg4
                      PxSP; 3 PxP

NO.118

1 Rg1, Kh5; 2 Qf5 ck, Kh4; 3 Pg3
   threat 2 QxP ck, Kh5; 3 Pg4

NO.119

1 Be1, Pa3; 2 Pd3 ck, Kd4; 3 Bd2, Pa2; 4 Pc3
       Kd4; 2 Pc3 ck, Kc4; 3 Bc2, Pa3; 4 Pd3
       Kb4; 2 Pd3 ck, Ka3; 3 Rb5, Ph5; 4 Bb4

NO.120

1 Qf5, SxB; 2 Qf4 ck, Re4; 3 Pe3
       PxB; 2 Sc2 ck, Kd5; 3 Pe4

12

Strategic Problems

AS PREVIOUSLY mentioned, problems in which the interest lies in the maneuvers leading up to the mates, rather than in the mating positions themselves, are often loosely termed "strategic" problems. Various examples of such problems will be discussed in this chapter. The thematic interest in strategic problems may lie principally either in the play of white or of black, or it may be in the interplay of both white and black men. In a brief survey of a few representative strategic themes the first to be examined will be some in which the play of white is dominant, and the defenses of black only incidental in bringing out points of the white maneuvers.

C. S. Kipping pioneered in experimenting with white self-unpinning by white interferences. A study of his problems led the author also to experiment with this theme, chiefly along the lines of multiple unpinnings activated by different black defenses. From the author's experiments a single example, No. 121, is here reproduced. This composition shows four lateral interference unpinnings of a white pawn by other white pawns, and in addition two withdrawal unpins by moves of the white king. In a problem of this type dual continuations following aimless moves by black are not regarded as such serious defects as they would be in some other types of compositions.

The mainplay in No. 122 was suggested by a problem composed by George Hume in collaboration with D. Pirnie, published in 1923, in which the white queen makes a lateral withdrawal move (Appendix A10). Note that problem 122 is a waiter, in which the bishop must be withdrawn to a square where the black queen can not attack it and yet retain her guard on f5. The next position, No. 123, illustrates a form of *clearance* maneuver. White desires to play Bf6 when the bishop can be supported on that square by the king. Before the king can move to g7, however, the bishop must be moved to the other side of that square and the only place where he can be parked safely is on a1. This problem has only the mainplay and one variation, the latter being introduced so that 1 Bc3 cannot be played.

In a problem competition held by the British Chess Association at Bristol, England, in 1861, Frank Healey (*1828–1906*) won first prize with a three-mover in which the key was a clearance move by a rook, made for the sole purpose of clearing the first rank for the queen. At that time such a clearance was regarded as a strikingly novel idea and the problem became famous. Nowadays when a rook or bishop makes such a *pure* clearance move for a queen the problem is termed a *Bristol*. Some authorities hold that the queen should not stand originally anywhere on the line that is so cleared, but should move onto it afterward and then follow the course of the clearing piece. This is what takes place in Healey's problem. If this strict view is held any illustration of the Bristol theme will require at least three moves, and there can be no true two-move Bristols. Commonly, however, the pure

121

The Pittsburgh Post
November 7, 1926

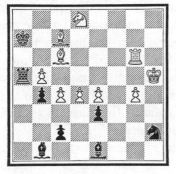

White mates in three moves

122

Die Schwalbe
November, 1928

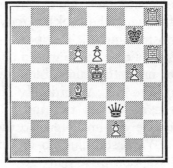

White mates in three moves

123

Skakbladet
July, 1930

White mates in three moves

124

The Empire Review
October, 1926

White mates in three moves

clearance move in itself is considered as constituting Bristol strategy.

In 1922 George Hume published a problem in which the clearing rook was obliged to make the clearance in two consecutive moves, because if the line were cleared at once black could temporarily shut off the queen from following the rook by moving a pawn onto the line and obstructing it. The position was constructed so that in such a case white would be left without any waiting move to mark time until black was obliged to move the pawn off the line. Accordingly Hume arranged the play so that the rook took two moves to make the clearance. This theme was aptly termed the *Hesitation Bristol*.

When standing on its initial square a pawn, by taking its option of moving two squares, can make a clearance for a queen or rook standing behind it. When a pawn moves but one square it is said to vacate the square on which it stood, but it does not clear a line, which must consist of at least two unoccupied squares. By moving two squares, however, a pawn may make a form of Bristol clearance. This is illustrated in problem 124, which may be termed a *Hesitation Pawn-Bristol*. White may play 1 Pc4 to allow the rook to move to c3, but the immediate advance of the pawn to the fourth rank does not lead to a mate if black plays 1 — — Ke4. The white pawn accordingly "hesitates" in its advance, viz., 1 Pc3. Now if 1 — — Ke4, then 2 Pe3, Kd5; 3 Pe4. If black, however, plays 1 — — Pe4, white completes the clearance with 2 Pc4, and after 2 — — Pe5, follows through with the rook, 3 Rc3.

Samuel Loyd developed a form of clearance which he called the *Annihilation theme*. In *Sam Loyd and His Chess Problems*, Alain C. White writes: "Annihilation usually occurs in problems where the chess-board is too small to allow an effective line clearance. . . . If there were a square beyond h8, to which the rook could move, it would allow a very pretty line clearance key." This second sentence referred to a problem by Loyd in which a white rook moves from h1 to h5 to be captured, or "annihilated," on that square by a black knight. The white queen follows the rook, and if the black knight moves again the file is cleared to h8 for the queen. In this theme the clearance can only become effective when black captures the white clearing piece, and then the white mating piece passes over the square on which the capture occurs after the black man vacates it, or makes a recapture on that square.

This theme suggested to the author another one which he has termed the *Angle theme*, but which is thematically different from the Annihilation theme, in that in the Angle theme a white rook or bishop makes a clearance move only secondarily for the purpose of affording a clearance for the queen, the primary purpose of the move being to threaten mate by making a second move at a right angle to the first. Should the rook or bishop be captured, however, on the square to which it has moved first, white recaptures with the queen, mating. In the Annihilation theme the clearance is *pure;* in the Angle theme the clearance is *impure*.

Problem 125 shows a diagonal setting of the Angle theme. White plays 1 Qe8, threatening 2 Bc6 ck. Should black defend by 1 —— Ra6, white continues 2 Ba4 threatening mate by 3 Bc2, a move at a right angle to the first move of the bishop. If black, however, captures the bishop on a4, the white queen recaptures, mating. Note incidentally that 1 —— Ra6 blocks that square so that black cannot later defend against 3 Bc2 by 2 —— Ba6. No. 126 shows an orthogonal version of the Angle theme, in which the thematic play is doubled.

Problem 127 illustrates what the author termed the *Substitution theme*. The queen's bishop substitutes for the queen to pin the knight; allowing the queen to substitute for the king's bishop in guarding the king's knight; and the king's bishop finally substitutes for the queen's knight in guarding g6; allowing the knight to mate. The four-move form was chosen to permit a sufficient number of substitutions to emphasize the theme.

The same theme is shown in No. 128 in the following line of play: 1 Bg5, Pc4; 2 Qd4, Pc3; 3 Ra1, etc. The bishop first substitutes for the queen, allowing the queen to substitute for the rook. The threat in this problem, 1 Bg5; 2 Bh3; 3 Qg4, is what is known as a *Turton clearance*. White's king's bishop makes a counter-clearance move so that the queen may move onto the diagonal in front of the bishop and be supported by it. The name is derived from a problem published by Henry Turton in 1856. This problem actually proved to be unsound and a few months later Samuel Loyd published a sound problem showing the theme, but the term "Turton" has persisted. The Turton clearance and the ensuing doubling of pieces on a line for attack is also shown in problem 152.

As explained in Chapter One, when a battery is formed by having the rear piece move into position from a square that is not on the line of attack, the rear piece is said to ambush itself behind the firing piece. One special way of forming an ambush is termed a *Herlin maneuver* after a problem published in 1845 by Theodor Herlin, who used the pseudonym, "The Anonymous Composer of Lille." In this maneuver the front man of a battery is first moved into position and then the rear piece brought *around*

125

L' Echiquier
September–October, 1930

White mates in three moves

126

V. Die Schwalbe
October, 1928
(April, 1930)

White mates in three moves

127

V. Originality Prize
Thirteenth Informal Tourney
The Westminster Gazette
May 1, 1926

White mates in four moves

128

V. The Westminster Gazette
April 24, 1926

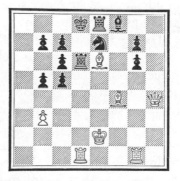

White mates in four moves

behind it. Thus instead of getting into position by cross-
ing the critical square, the rear piece goes around it, or
makes a *pericritical play*, as it is technically termed. This
will be readily understood by referring to problem 129.
First the rook moves to the critical square, 1 Rd3; then
follows 1 — — PxP; 2 Qa2, Pe2; 3 QxP, the queen ambushing herself behind the rook. In this problem the
maneuver is doubled, for if 1 — — Pf3; then 2 Qa1, Pf2;
3 Qf1. A further refinement in this position is that the
queen can not make her first move until the rook has
cleared the "a" file, but this feature is not essential to the
theme.

An elaboration of the Herlin theme is shown in No. 130.
In this problem the pawn first clears the diagonal, and
then the rook must be moved out of the way before the
bishop can begin to make its pericritical maneuver. After
the bishop is in the attacking position the rook must be
moved off the firing line before the pawn battery can be
fired. In fact, the battery might be regarded as having
two front pieces, both of which must be moved before
mate can be effected. This problem is a good illustration
of a legitimate six-move setting, because the full six moves
are required to carry out the theme.

The next position, No. 131, is an example of triple consecutive anticipatory line-closings or shut-offs of black
pieces, combined with decoys of the black king. The consecutive moves of the rook shut off any possible defenses
by the bishops. The idea is not new since G. Ernst (*1876–
1938*) had previously published a similar problem in
which, however, the illustration of the theme was not
technically pure, and Walter Jacobs (*b. 1914*) had shown
the theme with a white bishop shutting off a black rook
(Appendix A11).

The next group of problems illustrates themes based

129

Die Schwalbe
November, 1930

White mates in four moves

130

Die Schwalbe
December, 1928

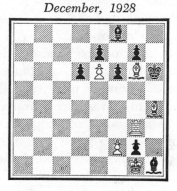

White mates in six moves

131

American Chess Bulletin
September–October, 1936

White mates in four moves

132

The Pittsburgh Post
April 25, 1926

White mates in three moves

primarily on the movements of the black men, particularly in their effects on each other in attempts to defend against white's attack. Such moves are sometimes termed *faulty maneuvers,* because while defeating one white threat they weaken black's defenses at some other point. Weenink in *The Chess Problem* subdivided such maneuvers into three groups, (1) blocking, (2) paralysis, and (3) interference, defining these terms as follows: "Blocking is limited to mean that a square is occupied by a piece so that another piece, usually of the same colour, cannot move to that square; Paralysis is limited to the case when the occupation of a square in this way, shuts up another piece of the same colour so that it cannot move; and Interference is limited to mean that a square is occupied so that another piece of the same colour cannot move across that square."

Blocking and interferences in two-movers were discussed in Chapter Four. Self-blocking by black rarely occurs in longer problems as a definite theme but usually as an incidental feature. Grimshaw and Nowotny interferences are essentially two-move themes, unless one or both of the black pieces involved are first to be decoyed over the critical square, in which case more moves are necessary. These two particular forms of black interference have been illustrated in the fourth chapter. There are other forms of black interference which always require at least three moves for their presentation, and examples of several of these types will be considered next. Paralysis also requires at least a three-move setting for adequate presentation, and illustrations of it appear in problems 144, 145 and 146.

The reverse of a black clearance move has popularly, even if not very accurately, been termed an anti-Bristol move. In an *anti-Bristol interference* two long range black pieces of the same kind (two rooks, or a bishop and a queen functioning as a bishop) are located on the same line and one or the other is induced to move toward its fellow so as to produce a form of interference. This is illustrated in No. 132. White plays 1 Bc3, threatening 2 Rf6 mate. Black can obstruct the guard of the bishop on f6 by playing a piece to e5, such as 1 — — Re2 – e5. Before this move both black rooks guarded e3, but after this move e3 is no longer directly guarded by the rook on e8. Accordingly if white continues 2 Se3 ck, the rook on e5 is forced to capture the knight and thus reopen the c3 – f6 diagonal, permitting white to mate. If black defends by 1 — — Re8 – e5, white plays 2 Se7 ck, etc.

The problem combines two anti-Bristol interferences, since both the bishop and queen also can move to e5, the white knights decoying them from that square in a similar fashion to the decoy of the rooks. This position is completely anticipated by a problem published by C. S. Kipping in 1921, with which the author was not familiar when he composed No. 132. The latter, however, is a more economical version of the theme, as it has three less men than Kipping used.

Where two black pieces of like motion moving on different but intersecting lines, mutually interfere on a critical square at the intersection of the lines, the interference is termed a *Plachutta interference,* after a problem published in 1858 by J. Plachutta. In the original form of the Plachutta interference a white man is sacrificed on the critical square, as in a Nowotny interference. Otto Wurzburg showed that the interference could be induced without the sacrifice, similarly to a Grimshaw interference, and Plachuttas without the sacrifice are therefore known as *Wurzburg-Plachuttas.*

Problem 133 is an ordinary Plachutta with the sacrifice

on the critical square. In the initial position e3 is guarded by the black queen and f6 is guarded by the black bishop. The critical square, where the lines of guard intersect, is d4. The key is 1 Pd4, threatening immediate mate, both by 2 Se3 and Sf6. If 1 — — QxPd4, white continues 2 Sf6 ck. The queen has interfered with the bishop's guard of f6, and so black is obliged to capture the knight with the queen, permitting mate by 3 Se3. If, on the other hand, 1 — — BxP; then 2 Se3 ck, BxS; 3 Sf6. This problem actually doubles the theme, since in addition to the diagonal Plachutta there is also an orthogonal Plachutta. After the first move has been made the position is such that white may be considered to have offered the pawn on e6 as a sacrifice, equally as well as the one on d4. So if 1 — — QxPd6; the continuation is 2 Se3 ck, QxS; 3 Sf6. If 1 — — RxP; 2 Sf6 ck, RxS; 3 Se3.

No. 134 is a Wurzburg-Plachutta. Instead of forcing an interference between the rooks by sacrificing a man on d6, the critical square, white brings about the interference by attacking black's king's rook with the bishop, 1 Bh4. If 1 — — Rf6 – d6; 2 RxKP ck, RxR; 3 Sc6. If black guards the king's rook with his other rook, 1 — — Rd7 – d6; then 2 Sc6 ck, RxS; 3 RxKP. This problem doubles the theme, since the black queen functions as a rook and e6 also is a critical square. Thus, 1 — — Re6; 2 Pe3 ck, RxP; 3 Sc6, and if 1 — — Qe6; then 2 Sc6 ck, QxS; 3 Pe3.

When the interference between two pieces of like motion, instead of being mutual, is restricted to the moves of one of the pair it is known as a *Holzhausen interference,* after Baron Walther von Holzhausen (*1876–1935*). One such interference occurs incidentally in No. 134 when black plays 1 — — Qe7, the queen interfering with the bishop's guard on the rook. Now if 2 BxR ck, black

133

The Chess Amateur
April, 1930

White mates in three moves

134

V. The Western Morning
News and Daily Gazette
July 10, 1937

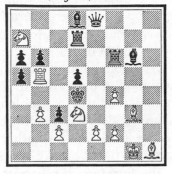

White mates in three moves

135

V. British Chess Magazine
September, 1944
(American Chess Bulletin
January–February, 1945)

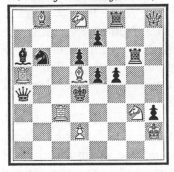

White mates in three moves

136

The Observer
April 25, 1926

White mates in three moves

is obliged to recapture with the queen instead of with the bishop, 2 — — QxR; 3 Pe3.

Although the term Wurzburg-Plachutta was originally applied to orthogonal interferences between two rooks (or a rook and a queen functioning as a rook), a similar mutual interference, without sacrifice, can occur between a bishop and queen operating on intersecting diagonals. For convenience this form of interference may be called a diagonal Wurzburg-Plachutta.

Orthogonal and diagonal Wurzburg-Plachuttas may be combined in one position. The pioneer illustration of this combination was a problem by Dr. Henry Wald Bettmann (*1868–1935*), published as No. 63 in *Tasks and Echoes* (1915). The author has composed a half-dozen examples based on two types of constructive mechanisms. In the first type the two pairs of interferences are motivated by a threat of check which in itself has no thematic relationship to the maneuvers. This type is shown in problem 135. Furthermore, the two pairs of mutual interferences have no relation to each other, but are defenses because they shut off lines for white pieces. Either rook moving to f6 prevents the white queen playing 2 QxKP, but interferes with the other black rook. 1 — — Qb5 or 1 — — Bb5 cuts off the rook's guard on e5 rendering the threat ineffective. This is a relatively simple method of combining orthogonal and diagonal Wurzburg-Plachuttas in one position. A more complex and more thematic method is shown in problem 136.

The key to No. 136 is 1 Pc5, threatening 2 Pc6, which would produce a Nowotny interference between black's queen's rook and bishop. To avoid the possibility of this interference black may move the rook across the critical square c6 to d6. The latter square, however, is the critical one for the interference between the rooks in an orthogo-

137

The Pittsburgh Post
May 16, 1926

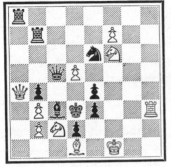

White mates in three moves

138

The Chess Correspondent
May–June, 1944

White mates in three moves

139

V. British Chess Magazine
July, 1944

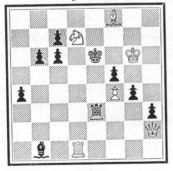

White mates in three moves

140

V. L' Echiquier
August, 1929

White mates in three moves

nal Wurzburg-Plachutta. Instead of moving the rook black may play the bishop across c6 to e4. This square, e4, is the critical square in a diagonal Wurzburg-Plachutta interference between the bishop and the queen. The fact that white's threat affects one member of each pair of pieces that take part in the Plachutta interferences, gives the play in this problem much more thematic unity than in a problem constructed like No. 135. Note finally that No. 136 also has a Holzhausen interference when black plays 1 — — Qd3; the queen interfering with the rook's guard on d2.

In problem 137 a diagonal Wurzburg-Plachutta is combined with Holzhausen interferences by the queen on each of the rooks.

All of the Wurzburg-Plachuttas shown in this chapter have second move threats, but it is possible to present a Wurzburg-Plachutta in a waiting move setting as will be seen by referring to the prize-winner by V. Kukainis, given in the Appendix as A12.

The next position, No. 138, was composed as an example of a *Brunner-Plachutta interference*, named after a problem published in 1912 by the Swiss composer, Eric Brunner (*1885–1938*). In this type of problem there is an interference between a rook and a bishop like a Nowotny, followed by decoys and mates as in Plachutta play. Brian Harley, in *Mate in Three Moves,* prefers to call the theme *Brunner-Nowotny.* The solution of No. 138 runs: 1 Sd5, BxS; 2 QxP ck, Bc4; 3 Qh5, and 1 — — RxS; 2 QxS ck, Re5; 3 Qa2.

In problem 139 no white man is sacrificed on the interference square and the black interferences are like a Grimshaw rather than a Nowotny. So the theme of No. 139 may be called a *Brunner-Grimshaw.*

Problem 140 shows a form of black interference which

141

*First Prize Three-Mover
Third Quarter, 1931
Die Schwalbe*

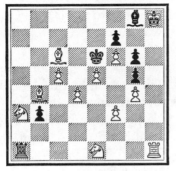

White mates in three moves

142

*L' Echiquier
January–February, 1932*

White mates in three moves

143

*The Observer
July 19, 1931*

White mates in three moves

144

*The Observer
April 12, 1931*

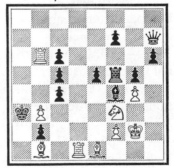

White mates in three moves

the author believes was first illustrated in this composition. The black queen is decoyed along the diagonal
to capture the knight at f6. Then the black bishop is
forced to e5 and held there by a pin, thus interfering
with the queen's potential return along the diagonal. This
allows white to release the pin on the black queen and
use the pinning piece, the white queen, to mate by 3 Qb4.

Valve play in two-movers was discussed in Chapter
Four. Naturally there is a wider scope for such play in
problems of greater length which permit the development of strategic maneuvers. The last eight problems in
this chapter illustrate various valve themes in three-move
settings. No. 141 shows the valve piece, the black bishop,
operating at the maximum possible distance from the
piece that it affects, the black rook. The valve defense
1 — — Bh7 permits white to retort 2 Sd3. Three valve
moves are made by a pawn in No. 142, each of them
leading to a different second-move continuation by the
white king. Two of these may be termed *anticipatory
valves* because they do not close an immediate line for
the black queen, but do close lines which otherwise would
be open after second-move plays. Thus if 1 — — Qc8 the
c8 – h3 diagonal is open, but it will be closed after
1 — — Pe6. Likewise after 1 — — Qb8 the b8 – h2 diagonal is open, but it will be closed after 1 — — Pe5.

Problem 143 combines two anticipatory valve variations with anticipatory shut-offs by white of the black
rook. The solution runs 1 Kg2, threat 2 SxSP, etc. If
1 — — Pb6; 2 Be7. The black pawn has made 2 — — Ra6
ineffective and the white bishop now prevents 2 — — Rf7.
If 1 — — Pb5; 2 Pe5. Here the black pawn renders use-
less 2 — — Ra5 and the white pawn does the same for
2 — — Re7.

The form of faulty maneuver classified as paralysis by

145

V. First Commended
Informal Tourney
January–June, 1931
British Chess Magazine

White mates in three moves

146

Third Prize
Second International Tourney
Skakbladet
July, 1931

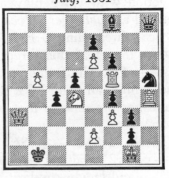

White mates in three moves

147

The Western Morning News
January 30, 1932

White mates in three moves

148

Third Honorable Mention
Informal Tourney
January–June, 1932
British Chess Magazine

White mates in three moves

Weenink was mentioned earlier in this chapter. Johannes Seeberger (*1843–1879*) illustrated this maneuver in a four-mover published in 1860 and so such play is termed a *Seeberger interference*. In problems 144, 145, and 146 this paralyzing, or bottling up, of pieces is shown in conjunction with valve play and such valves may be described as *Seeberger valves*. Thus in No. 144 white plays 1 Bc3, threatening 2 Bc2, and black has two thematic moves to defeat this threat. These are 1 — — Rf6 and 1 — — Pf6. The former paralyzes the bishop's pawn so that white can mate by 2 Rd7 and 3 Ra7, and the latter paralyzes the rook so that white can mate by 2 Se1 and 3 Sc2.

In No. 145, 1 — — Sc2 paralyzes the pawn c3, and 1 — — Pc2 paralyzes the knight a3. In No. 146 the black bishop and knight similarly paralyze each other by moving to g7. The solver will notice that in all these positions the maneuver is doubled by having two men mutually paralyze each other in the thematic variations.

In addition to valves where black men close and open lines for other black pieces, there can be white-black valves, as already mentioned in Chapter Four, in which a black man while closing one line for a white piece opens another line for it. Where the terms *white-black* and *black-white* are used, the color first mentioned is the one affected by the maneuver, which is executed by a man of the color mentioned last.

Problem 147 has three black pieces which can close the line c8 – h8 to prevent the white queen from reaching h8, but each of these moves opens another line of attack for her. Finally, in No. 148 there are two consecutive white-black valves in the main-play: 1 Rg4, Bb8; 2 Ra3, Bb3; 3 RxR. Incidentally this problem has a good try, 1 QRg8, met only by the subtle defense, 1 — — Bb6.

SOLUTIONS

NO.121

1 Bb7, Bc3;   2 Pc5, *threat* 3 Pb6

    Pc1=Q;   2 Pd5

       Bg3;   2 Pe5

       Bh4;   2 Pg5

       SxP;   2 KxS

       Sf1;   2 Kh6

NO.122

1 Ba1, Qc3 ck; 2 Kf5

NO.123

1 Ba1, *threat* 2 Kg7; 3 Bf6

       PxP; 2 Sc3

NO.124

1 Pc3, Pe4; 2 Pc4, Pe5; 3 Rc3

    Ke4; 2 Pe3, Kd5; 3 Pe4

NO.125

1 Qe8, *threat* 2 Bc6 ck

        Ra6; 2 Ba4, *threat* 3 Bc2

            RxB; 3 QxR

NO.126

1 Qg7, *threat* 2 Rg1, *threat* 3 Rd1

             PxR; 3 Qxg1

        Pa4; 2 Ra7, *threat* 3 RxPa4

             BxR; 3 QxB

NO.127

1 Be3; 2 Qd1; 3 Bf5; 4 Sg8

NO.128

1 Bg5, *threat* 2 Bh3;   3 Qg4; 4 Qc8

        Pc4; 2 Qd4, Pc3; 3 Ra1; 4 Ra8

NO.129

1 Rd3, PxP; *2* Qa2, Pe2; *3* QxP, KxP; *4* Ra3
          Pf3; *2* Qa1, Pf2; *3* Qf1, KxP; *4* Ra3

NO.130

1 Pf4, Pf5; *2* Rg5, Pd5; *3* Be1, Pd4; *4* Bd2, Pd3; *5* Rg4, PxR;
                                                        6 Pf5

NO.131

1 Rg3, Kh2; *2* Rg4, Kh3; *3* Rg5, Kh4; *4* Kg6

NO.132

1 Bc3, Re2—e5; *2* Se3 ck
          Re8—e5; *2* Se7 ck
          Be5; *2* Sd6 ck
          Qe5; *2* Sg3 ck

NO.133

1 Pd4, QxQP; *2* Sf6 ck
          BxP; *2* Se3 ck
          QxKP; *2* Se3 ck
          RxP; *2* Sf6 ck

NO.134

1 Bh4, *threat* *2* BxR ck
          Rf6—d6; *2* RxQP ck
          Rd7—d6; *2* Sc6 ck
          Re6; *2* Pe3 ck
          Qe6; *2* Sc6 ck
          Qe7; *2* BxR ck

NO.135

1 Bg2, *threat* *2* QxPe5 ck
          Qb5; *2* Se2 ck
          Bb5; *2* Sc6 ck
          Rf8—f6; *2* Se6 ck
          Rg6—f6; *2* SxP ck

NO.136

1 Pc5, *threat* *2* Pc6
          QRd6; *2* QxQP ck
          KRd6; *2* Se6 ck
          Be4; *2* RxBP ck
          Qe4; *2* QxBP ck
          Qd3; *2* QxQP ck

NO.137

1 Sd7, *threat* *2* SxQ ck
          Bd4; *2* RxP ck
          Qd4; *2* Se5 ck
          Qb6; *2* Qb5 ck
          Qa7; *2* Qa6 ck

NO.138
1 Sd5, *threat* 2 Sf4 ck

 BxS; 2 QxP ck, Bc4; 3 Qh5

 RxS; 2 QxS ck, Re5; 3 Qa2

 BxQ; 2 KxS

NO.139
1 Sf6, *threat* 2 Rd8

 Bd3; 2 Qa2 ck, Bc4; 3 QxB

 Rd3; 2 Qe2 ck, Re3; 3 Qc4

NO.140
1 Qf8, QxS; 2 Bc7 ck, Be5; 3 Qb4

NO.141
1 Bd2, *threat* 2 Sc4

 Bh7; 2 Sd3

 Rc1; 2 Sb5

 RxKS; 2 RxR

NO.142
1 Rb5, *threat* 2 Bb4 ck

 Te0; 2 Kh3

 Pe5; 2 Kg3

 PxP; 2 Kf3

NO.143
1 Kg2, *threat* 2 SxSP

 Pb6; 2 Be7

 Pb5; 2 Pe6

NO.144
1 Bc3, *threat* 2 Bc2

 Rf6; 2 Rd7

 Pf6; 2 Se1

NO.145
1 Se2, *threat* 2 Sf4

 Sc2; 2 Bh4

 Pc2; 2 Pa7

NO.146
1 Pb6, *threat* 2 RxQP

 Bg7; 2 KxP

 Sg7; 2 Pb7

NO.147
1 Qc8, *threat* 2 Qh8 ck

 QSd8; 2 QxP

 Bd8; 2 Qc3 ck

 KSd8; 2 QxQB

NO.148
1 Rg4, *threat* 2 QRg8

 Bb8; 2 Ra3, Bb3; 3 RxR

13

Pawn Promotion Themes

MANY interesting effects may be obtained by the promotion of pawns, especially where the promotion is to some piece other than a queen. In the case of white, promotions to a rook or to a bishop are to avoid the possibility of a stalemate position. Promotions to a knight are also sometimes made for that reason, but more frequently they are for the purpose of controlling squares that would not be reached by a queen.

Conversely, black promotions to a rook or to a bishop are to threaten stalemate as a defense. Promotions to a knight are to defend squares which could not be defended by a queen, although it is possible to construct positions where a promotion to a knight would threaten stalemate.

Promotions to a rook or bishop, instead of to a queen, are known as minor promotions or *under-promotions*. The promotion to a knight is not always so termed, since it can control squares which a queen cannot. Promotions to rook or bishop cannot be illustrated in two-move form, because a stalemate position, to be set up by black or to be avoided by white, requires at least a three-mover for its development. Accordingly in two-movers it is possible only to differentiate between promotions to queen or knight.

149

The Weekly Westminster
October 24, 1925

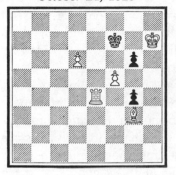

White mates in three moves

150

Chess Review
September, 1936

White mates in four moves

151

Commended
Eleventh Informal Tourney
The Weekly Westminster
January 17, 1925

White mates in four moves

152

Chemnitzer Tageblatt und
Anzeiger
August 29, 1926

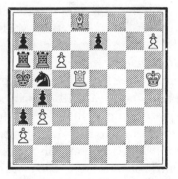

White mates in four moves

Several three-move problems have been composed in which a white pawn is promoted to each of the four pieces, according to black's defensive play. The first illustrative problem in this chapter shows the promotion of a pawn to three different pieces, rook, knight and queen, and its chief merit lies in the extreme lightness of the setting, only a total of eight men being employed. In this particular position a possible stalemate is avoided by promoting the pawn to a rook.

In the next problem there are only two lines of play, one leading to a promotion to bishop to avoid stalemate and the other involving a promotion to knight for attacking purposes, but the resulting mates in both lines are models. Note that in the first line the promotion gives white two queen's bishops and in the second line three knights, an intentionally Puckish effect.

Problem 151 illustrates an under-promotion to a rook to form an ambush and to force the black king to expose himself by making him capture the knight. In the second line of play in this composition the rooks interchange their functions.

The next three positions show what is known as *Indian* strategy in connection with pawn promotion play. In 1845 a problem was published in the *Chess Player's Chronicle*, composed by a young clergyman living in India, Henry Augustus Loveday (*1815–1848*), where white made a withdrawal of a piece across a critical square onto which a white masking piece afterward moved to avoid stalemating black. The composition was published anonymously and was called the "Indian problem." Because the idea was so novel at the time, the position became famous, although it actually was not sound, and the term *Indian* has come to be applied generally to positions where a white piece withdraws over

153

V. American Chess Bulletin
January, 1926

White mates in five moves

154

The Pittsburgh Post
January 18, 1925

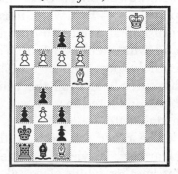

White mates in four moves

155

The Gambit of the Missouri
Pacific, St. Louis Chess Club
November, 1924

White mates in three moves

156

Commended
Eleventh Informal Tourney
The Weekly Westminster
January 24, 1925

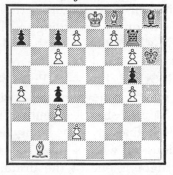

White mates in four moves

a critical square so that its guard may be shut off, by another white man, to avoid a stalemate.

An examination of problem 152 may make this explanation easier to understand. The key is 1 Rg5; the rook withdrawing over the critical square e5. Should black play 1 — — Pe6, white must promote the rook's pawn to a bishop and not to a queen. Black continues 2 — — Pe5 and white replies 3 BxP. This might be regarded as not entirely pure Indian strategy because the black pawn has already shut off the white rook, but if the pawn had been promoted to a queen, 3 QxP would have resulted in a stalemate.

The other variation of this problem shows a Turton clearance, in which a white piece withdraws in order to let another white piece take a position in front of it for the purpose of attack. This is known as *Turton doubling* and has already been described in connection with problem 128. Thus if black plays 1 — — Pe5, the continuation is 2 Ph8=Q, Pe4; 3 Qe5 (the Turton doubling), Pe3; 4 QxS.

No. 153 shows the Indian maneuver doubled in two lines of play, requiring the promotion of a pawn to rook or to queen according to black's play. The solution runs: 1 Ba7 (critical move), Pb4; 2 Ph8=R, Pb3; 3 Rb8, Pb2; 4 Rb6 (masking move on the critical square), KxS; 5 Rb6xPb2. 1 — — PxP; 2 Ph8=Q, Pa3; 3 Qa1, Pa2; 4 Rb6 (masking move on the critical square), KxS; 5 Rb2. No. 154 also shows a double Indian, the masking pieces in both lines of play being derived from different promotions of white's queen's pawn. Here the promotion to knight is one of the instances where such a promotion occurs for the primary purpose of avoiding stalemate, although the knight is also needed to guard a4 in the mating position.

157

The Staten Islander
February 4, 1925

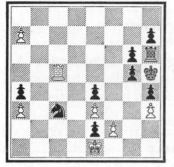

White mates in three moves

158

The Pittsburgh Post
November 16, 1924

White mates in three moves

159

Chemnitzer Tageblatt und
Anzeiger
February 1, 1925

White mates in three moves

160

Honor Problem
Chess Review
July, 1936

White mates in three moves

Problem 155 is not strategically so interesting as the more complicated positions in this chapter, but it is included for the novelty of its keymove. For the key a piece occupies the square on which the promotion is subsequently to take place and at first glance it would seem likely that this square should be left unoccupied. The next two positions show minor promotions to rook and to bishop respectively in combination with en passant pawn captures, No. 156 being the more interesting of the two strategically. Note the masking play in the secondary line of this problem, which is analogous to that in the primary line.

The *grab theme* is illustrated in No. 158. In its more simple forms this theme is regarded as too "brutal" to have much appeal. In the grab theme a black man must be run down and captured before mate can be effected. In this particular position the author endeavors to introduce a little subtlety by having two semi-free black pieces. Only one of the knights is needed to guard the black pawn so that either knight alone seems free to move. If white can capture one of the knights, however, the other will be obliged to move and relinquish its guard on the pawn. The promotion of the pawn to a knight completes the guard of all the squares available to the black knights.

In Chapter Six the half-pin was examined in relation to its use in two-movers, although it can of course occur in three-movers (compare No. 165) or longer problems. This potential pinning of a black man may be extended to a *third-pin,* and theoretically even further. A third-pin requires at least a three-move setting for its illustration. In the latter days of the Good Companions some experiments were made with third-pins, but as a rule they prove too cumbersome for attractive effects. Problem 159 shows a third-pin in combination with grab play. Although this problem has a promotion key, the keymove is not thematic but really only incidental to the play. In fact the problem is given here merely as a sort of sequel to No. 158, and because of the rather amusing effect of having three white knights on the board.

To close the chapter an example of black promotions is given in No. 160, the promotion of the pawn to queen, bishop or knight, respectively leading to three different lines of play. A promotion to a rook has to be treated by white the same as a promotion to a queen. If black chooses a bishop, white cannot continue as he does when black selects a queen, since it would lead to a stalemate. The choice of the bishop, however, allows white to permit the black king to move to a2, which cannot be done when black takes a queen or a rook.

Very elaborate effects have been produced in an intensive study of the possibilities of combinations of black and white promotion play, particularly in self-mate form, which seems to be peculiarly adapted for such presentations. These studies culminated in the successful achievement of the "Babsontask" (Joseph Ney Babson, *1852–1929*), showing black pawn promotions on the same square to queen, rook, bishop or knight, countered by white pawn promotions on a single square to the same respective pieces. The first prize problem in the Babsontask contest, by Dr. Henry Wald Bettmann is reproduced in the Appendix as No. A13.

SOLUTIONS

NO.149　　*1* Pd7, Pg5;　2 Pd8=R, Kf6;　　3 Rf8

　　　　　　　　PxP;　2 Pd8=S ck, Kf6;　3 Bh4

　　　　　　　　Kf6;　2 Pd8=Q ck, KxP;　3 Re5

NO.150   1 Ke4, PxP; 2 Pf7, Pe5;   3 Pf8=B, Kg8;   4 Sf6
                  Kg8; 2 PxP ck, Kh7; 3 Pf8=S ck, Kg8; 4 Pf7

NO.151   *1* Pg8=R, Pe5; 2 Rg3, Pe4;   3 Re3, KxS; 4 Re1
                  PxP; 2 Rg8−b8, Pf4; 3 RxP, KxS; 4 Rf1

NO.152   *1* Rg5, Pe6; 2 Ph8=B, Pe5; 3 BxP, S any; 4 BxS
                  Pe5; 2 Ph8=Q, Pe4; 3 Qe5, Pe3;   4 QxS

NO.153   *1* Ba7, Pb4; 2 Ph8=R, Pb3; 3 Rb8, Pb2; 4 Rb6, KxS;
                                                            5 Rb6xPb2
                  PxP; 2 Ph8=Q, Pa3; 3 Qa1, Pa2; 4 Rb6, KxS;
                                                            5 Rb2

NO.154   *1* Bf7, PxQP; 2 Pd8=R, Pd5; 3 RxP, KxP; 4 Ra5
                  PxSP; 2 Pd8́=S, Pb5; 3 Se6, KxP; 4 Sc5

NO.155   *1* Sb8, Ke7; 2 Sc6 ck, Kd7; 3 Pb8=S

NO.156   *1* Pd8=R, Pa5; 2 Pd4, PxPep; 3 RxP, KxP; 4 Rd6
                  Pa6; 2 Rd4, Pa5;   3 Re4, KxP; 4 Re6

NO.157   *1* Pa8=B, Sd5; 2 BxS, *etc.*
                  Sd1; 2 Pf4, *etc.*

NO.158   *1* Ph8=S, *etc.*
NO.159   *1* Pd8=S, *etc.*

NO.160   *1* Qc4, Pa1=Q; 2 Qb3, any;   3 Rc1
                  Pa1=B; 2 QxP ck, Ka2; 3 Ra3
                  Pa1=S; 2 Ra3, Sb3;   3 QxP
                              Sc2;   3 Qa2

14

En Passant Pawn Captures

THE EN PASSANT capturing of pawns may lead to so many interesting forms of line opening and line obstruction that numerous problems have been composed to illustrate the thematic possibilities of this type of pawn capture. Under the title of *Running the Gauntlet*, Alain C. White devoted a volume of *The Christmas Series* to "A study of the capture of pawns en passant in chess problems." The introduction to the book, combined with the table of contents, developed a complete scheme for the classification of such problems. In this chapter, however, the reader will merely be shown a few examples of typical effects that result from such captures.

In the first example, No. 161, the pawn en passant capture, so far as the theme of the problem is concerned, is only one of several strategic elements. The key is 1 Pd4, threatening 2 Pd5, which would lead to a Nowotny interference between the rook and the bishop. If black endeavors to prevent this threat by playing 1 — — PxPep, the third rank is obstructed so that white can retort 2 PxB, without leaving his king open to check from the rook.

The next problem, No. 162, is a medley of line obstructions for black combined with line openings for white. It is not of a style of composition that the author commends, even though he occasionally has been guilty of perpetrating such affairs. The key is 1 Bc5, threatening 2 Pe4 ck, BxP; 3 KRxP. Black defends either by arranging for en passant captures of white's king's pawn or by actually blocking its advance. Thus, 1 — — Qd3; 2 Pe4 ck, PxPep; 3 QxQ, both rook and bishop being shut off by the capturing pawn. 1 — — Rd3; 2 Pe4 ck, PxPep; 3 QxB. 1 — — PxP; 2 Pe4 ck, PxPep; 3 Qh5. If black blocks the pawn by 1 — — Qe3, the continuation then is 2 Pc4 ck, PxPep; 3 Qb3. 1 — — Be3 also leads to thematic play, since white replies 2 SxQ threatening 3 Bc4, and if black plays 2 — — PxS, the pawn is decoyed so it can not defend against 3 Pc4 with an en passant capture. Although this position is in the nature of a task problem, it happens to have an excellent try, 1 Ke7, to which the defense is not immediately apparent.

Problem 163 shows how en passant pawn captures can readily be blended with other thematic features, which in this case are black half-pins. The key is 1 BxP, with the double threat of 2 Pc4 ck or 2 Pe4 ck. In the thematic defenses black sets up a half-pin formation, either on one or the other side of his king, by 1 — — Pb5 or 1 — — Sg5, with true half-pin mates ensuing, unless black elects to make en passant pawn captures.

The problems so far considered have en passant captures only of white pawns. The next two positions show such captures both of white and black pawns, and in each problem the thematic line of play is doubled. In No. 165, furthermore, the black pawns on d7 and e7 are initially half-pinned and the mates in the two thematic lines are true half-pin mates.

C. S. Kipping, who always was seeking some strategic novelty, suggested to the author the possibilities that might lie in en passant captures of a white pawn by each

161

The Observer
March 22, 1925

White mates in three moves

162

British Chess Magazine
January, 1926

White mates in three moves

163

The Western Morning News
and Mercury
September 11, 1926

White mates in three moves

164

American Chess Bulletin
May–June, 1938

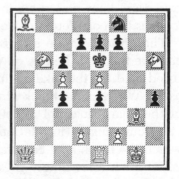

White mates in three moves

of a pair of half-pinned black pawns, the captures to be made on black's first move in a three-mover. Problems 166 and 167 are results of this suggestion. In illustrating this theme it will be seen that to make an en passant capture of the white pawn the black pawns must necessarily stand on the fourth rank, and if the black pawns are half-pinned the black king must likewise be on that rank. The black king, however, may have any one of four different positions in relation to the black pawns. He may be on the square adjacent to the nearest pawn, as in No. 167, or with one, two or three vacant squares between. These four positions are the only possible ones for the black king in this theme.

This is a convenient place to explain two technical terms used by composers who are making a systematic study of a theme. In a theme, such as the one shown in problems 166 and 167, where there is a necessarily definite relationship between the location of the critical square and the position of the black king, the various combinations of squares on which the theme can be illustrated are known as *spots* in the locus of the theme. The *locus* is the complete picture of all possible spots.

The critical square in this particular en passant pawn capture theme is the one on which the white pawn is captured, and for the sake of uniformity it may be regarded as c3. Whether the black king is on one or the other side of the board does not affect the relationships. There are only four squares, in relation to the critical square c3, on which the black king can stand. These squares are e4, f4, g4, and h4. Accordingly these four relations between the black king's position and the critical square, or four spots, constitute the complete locus of this theme. The loci of most themes are much less limited, since ordinarily there are many more possible spots.

165

V. Commended
Twelfth Informal Tourney
The Weekly Westminster
November 14, 1925
(British Chess Magazine
June, 1926)

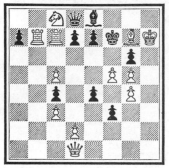

White mates in three moves

166

First Commended
Three-Move Section
Third C. C. L. A.
North American Tourney
C. C. L. A. Bulletin
April, 1939

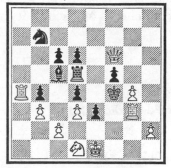

White mates In three moves

167

American Chess Bulletin
May–June, 1938

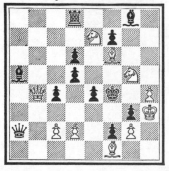

White mates in three moves

168

American Chess Bulletin
July–August, 1938

White mates in three moves

The final problem in this chapter, No. 168, is given to show an unusually peculiar effect of an en passant capture. A white pawn, although pinned diagonally, can capture a black pawn en passant. The result of the capture in this instance is to remove a line obstruction on an adjoining diagonal so that mate is given from a bishop which itself has not moved. In this particular line of play the effect is as though the white pawn gave successive discovered checks on each of its moves.

SOLUTIONS

NO.161
1 Pd4, PxPep;   2 PxB

NO.162
1 Bc5, *threat* 2 Pe4 ck, BxP;   3 KRxP
        Qd3;   2 Pe4 ck, PxPep;   3 QxQ
        Rd3;   2 Pe4 ck, PxPep;   3 QxB
        PxP;   2 Pe4 ck, PxPep;   3 Qh5
        Qe3;   2 Pc4 ck, PxPep;   3 Qb3
        Be3;   2 SxQ, PxS;   3 Pc4

NO.163
1 BxP, Pb5;   2 Pc4 ck, PxPep;   3 Pe4
    Sg5;   2 Pe4 ck, PxPep;   3 Pc4

NO.164
1 Pd4, BPxPep;   2 Qa2 ck, Pd5;   3 BPxPep
    KPxPep;   2 Pf4, Pf5;   3 PxPep

NO.165
1 Pd4, BPxPep;   2 Qb3 ck, Pd5;   3 PxPep
    KPxPep;   2 Qe1, Pe5;   3 PxPep

NO.166

1 Pc4, *threat* 2 PxR

    SPxPep; 2 SxKP

    QPxPep; 2 SxBP

NO.167

1 Pd4, *threat* 2 Se6 ck

    BPxPep; 2 Sf3

    KPxPep; 2 BxP

NO.168

1 Pc6, *threat* 2 Re8 ck

    Qe7 ck; 2 Pg5 ck, Pf5; 3 PxPep

15

Castling Themes

IN THE past many problem authorities and composers have objected to castling in problems on the ground that the right to castle can never be proved in any given initial problem position. Some have suggested as a compromise that black, being the defensive player, should be allowed the privilege but that it should be denied to white. The commonsense viewpoint is that inasmuch as castling takes place in almost every game that is played and because it is a move with peculiar positional consequences, composers should exploit its problemistic possibilities.

From a practical point of view castling should not lead to any misunderstanding for the solver, since in the majority of castling problems the setting immediately suggests that castling is to take place at some time during the course of the solution.

More of the peculiar properties of the castling move affect the play of white than they do that of black. Problems exploiting the castling move for the benefit of white are commonly called "white castlers," and the first three problems in this chapter illustrate some of the special effects of this move. Castling, for instance, permits the white king simultaneously to vacate his home square so that another man may move onto it, and to move two

169

Die Schwalbe
April, 1929

White mates in three moves

170

V. The Western Morning
News
March 30, 1929
(New York Evening Post
January 7, 1933)

White mates in three moves

171

Honorable Mention
Informal Tourney
The Chess Amateur
Fairy Section
May, 1929

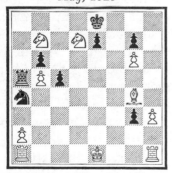

White mates in three moves

172

L' Echiquier
June, 1929

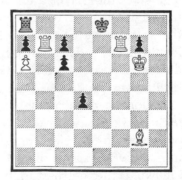

White mates in three moves

squares away to another black square, where he will be safe from attack. In problem 169 this maneuver is doubled.

In No. 170 the white king again vacates his home square so that the knight may move there to mate. After the key is made there are five different squares to which the king threatens to move. There are, however, five distinct black defenses which limit the white king's movement to each of these squares in turn. Five vacating moves by the white king were previously shown in a problem by Alain White which appeared in 1928 as the frontispiece in *The Properties of Castling*, and which is reproduced in the Appendix as No. A14.

After the keymove is made in problem 171, white can threaten mate by moving a rook either to d1 or to f1, but at the same time he has to make certain that his king will not be subject to attack. Therefore, according to black's defenses white plays 2 Rd1 or 2 Rf1 or castles on one side or on the other. A joint composition by Kipping and Hume, showing these features, was published in *The Chess Amateur* in October, 1922. Mr. White, in commenting upon this latter problem, remarks: "the castling privilege gives the player a chance to make a particular move in two ways. Thus White can move 1 Rf1, or he may make the same move as a part of castling. The rook move is identical in the two cases, but the result may be entirely distinct. There is no other means in chess to get two identical moves producing differentiated results."

Although white castling affords the greater possibilities for unusual strategic effects, black castling gives an opportunity to develop unusual mating positions. These frequently are in the nature of echoes, one thematic line following the castling defense and the other line the movement of the rook up to the king without castling. In

173

British Chess Magazine
February, 1931

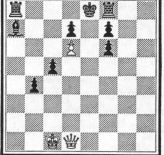

White mates in three moves

174

The Observer
February 5, 1933

White mates in three moves

175

V. The Observer
June 29, 1930
(Newark Evening News
October 28, 1930)

White mates in three moves

176

Skakbladet
December, 1930

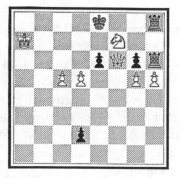

White mates in three moves

No. 172, for example, the rook is pinned on d7 in the mates in each of the two thematic lines, but in one case the black king is on c8 while in the other he remains on e8. These mates are not models. The next five problems, however, were composed specifically for the model mating positions, although two of them also show decoy strategy leading to the thematic mates.

In No. 173 there are three model mates, with the black king on e8, d8 and c8 respectively. The problem was composed to show three model mates with a minimum white mating force, which consists of the queen and pawn, since the white king takes no part in the mates, but is placed on c1 to obviate dual continuations despite the double threat. There are dual continuations only after two rook moves. The solution runs: 1 Qf3, Rh8; 2 QxR ck, Bb8; 3 QxB. 1 — — Bb6; 2 Qe4 ck, Kd8; 3 QxR. 1 — — 0 – 0 – 0; 2 Qa8 ck, Bb8; 3 Qa6.

No. 174 shows symmetrically echoed model mates after black self-blocking on d8; one mate follows castling by black and the other mate the move of the black rook to d8 without castling. In each of these variations the white queen is sacrificed to effect the decoy of a black man. The same strategy is followed in problem 175. In this composition the thematic mates may be regarded as echoes, since in one the rook mates while the knight acts as a guard, and in the second mate their functions are reversed. The author worked on-and-off this position for about a year to get a satisfactory setting, and then when he finally submitted it for publication he omitted the pawn on e4, thinking it was unnecessary, but this omission permitted a cook by 1 Qa4.

The most elaborate of these castling echoes is shown in problem 176. One line leading to the echoed mate follows white's threat, while the second line follows the castling

177

The Problemist
Fairy Chess Supplement
October, 1931

White mates in three moves

178

The Chess Amateur
Fairy Section
May, 1929

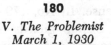

White mates in four moves

179

V. The Problemist
October 19, 1929

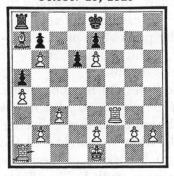

White mates in four moves

180

V. The Problemist
March 1, 1930

White mates in four moves

defense. There is also practically a third echo if black plays 1 — — KPxP. The solution is 1 Kb6, threat 2 Sd6 ck, Kd7; 3 QPxP. 1 — — 0 – 0; 2 SxR ck, Kh7; 3 RPxP. 1 — — KPxP; 2 Sd6 ck, Kd7; 3 Pc6. Three model mates occur in problem 177, two involving the queening of white's king's rook's pawn and the third following the queening of white's queen's rook's pawn, the latter mate being a pin-model.

The next two positions look like "black castlers," but should black be permitted to castle in either one there would be no mate. Accordingly in each instance the theme of the problem is the prevention of castling. This is accomplished in No. 178 by 1 Sd7, forcing the rook to move. White then plays 2 Se5, a *switchback*, a term applied when a piece returns to its initial square. Black, however, can not undo the effect of his rook move by 2 — — Rh8, and so white can now mate in two moves with the rook, since black no longer has castling available as a defense. In No. 179 black can castle even though the white bishop guards b8, since the black king does not have to pass over a guarded square, but by sacrificing the bishop on b8 white prevents the castling defense. This problem, besides illustrating the prevention of black castling, is also a "white castler," white either castling or playing Kd2 according to black's defenses.

Problem 180 is not a "castler" despite its appearance. It was reproduced in White's *Problems By My Friends* as No. 106, and Mr. Hume in the notes to that collection commented on it thus: "While what we might call the positive theme here is the mutual masking of the white rook and bishop in the two variations with Indian effects, there is also a negative theme in that White must restrain his inclination to castle on his first move, because the square g1 is required for the bishop to occupy when it makes its critical move. In other words, castling is a good try."

SOLUTIONS

NO.169
1 Bf2, *threat* 2 0 – 0
      Bb5; 2 0 – 0 – 0

NO.170
1 Bf5, Qg7, 8; 2 0 – 0
      Se5; 2 0 – 0 – 0
      Qd6; 2 Kf1
      Qh6; 2 Kd1
      SxP; 2 Kd2

NO.171
1 Be6, Sb2; 2 0 – 0
      Pg2; 2 0 – 0 – 0
      Sc3; 2 Rf1
      RxP; 2 Rd1

NO.172
1 Rb3, 0 – 0 – 0; 2 Bh3 ck
      Rd8; 2 BxP ck

NO.173
1 Qf3, Rh8; 2 QxR ck, Bb8; 3 QxB
      Bb6; 2 Qe4 ck, Kd8; 3 QxR
      0 – 0 – 0; 2 Qa8 ck, Bb8; 3 Qa6

NO.174
1 QxRP, 0 – 0 – 0; 2 QxBP ck, RxQ; 3 Ba6
             Rd8; 2 Qe6 ck, PxQ;   3 Bh5

NO.175
1 Qg1, 0 – 0 – 0; 2 Qa7, SxQ; 3 RxP
         Rd8; 2 Qd4, SxQ; 3 SxP

NO.176
1 Kb6, *threat* 2 Sd6 ck, Kd7; 3 QPxP
           0 – 0; 2 SxR ck, Kh7; 3 RPxP
      KPxP; 2 Sd6 ck, Kd7; 3 Pc6

NO.177

1 Qe3, Pg1=Q;	2 Ph8=Q ck (*threat*), Ke7;	3 Pf6		
Ke7;	2 Qg5 ck, Kf8;		3 Ph8=Q	
0 – 0 – 0;	2 Pa8=Q ck, Sb8;		3 Qc1	

NO.178

1 Sd7, Rg8, f8; 2 Se5, any; 3 Rd1

NO.179

1 Bb8, Pd5 *or* Ra6;	2 0 – 0 – 0, any;	3 QRf1
RxB;	2 Kd2, any;	3 QRf1

NO.180

1 Rf1, Pd3; 2 Bg1, Pg6; 3 Rf2
Pg6; 2 Rf6, Pd3; 3 Bd6

16

The White Rooks

JUST as some composers have experimented with special types of chess moves, as discussed in the last three chapters, composers also have experimented with the construction of problems using only certain types of men, especially in respect to the white forces. The little book that Mr. White issued as the 1909 volume of *The Christmas Series* was called *Knights and Bishops* and contained a hundred problems where white had only knights and bishops, in addition to the king and pawns. The next year he published *The White Rooks*, a collection of 274 compositions where the white forces were limited to the king, rooks, and pawns.

This book aroused so much interest in white rook problems that Mr. White brought out another volume on the same subject the very next year (1911). This was entitled *More White Rooks* and it contained not only numerous additional published problems brought to Mr. White's attention since the publication of the first rook book, but also many original contributions whose composition had been inspired by that volume. *More White Rooks* contained 400 positions.

The study of these two volumes by the author nearly fifteen years later, led him to compose over half a hundred such problems, of which eight examples are given in this chapter to show the wide possibilities of so apparently restricted materials as rooks, pawns, and the king. These men by themselves are best adapted for presentations of themes in three-movers, or longer problems, because some maneuvering usually is necessary to effect mate. The composition of No. 181 was somewhat in the nature of a stunt, to show that it was possible to construct a truly thematic two-mover with white rooks, pawns, and king only. In other respects such a position could not compare favorably with one in which the composer was unrestricted in his use of men.

In the three- and four-move field, however, beautiful effects can be secured with these men. The echoed pawn mate in No. 182, for instance, could not be improved by the employment of a greater variety of men. Problem 183 illustrates sacrificial strategy, both on white's first and second moves.

On page 91 of *More White Rooks,* Mr. White remarked: "So far I have seen no sound ambuscade of a rook behind three white pawns. The task appears to be a most difficult one." This statement led the author to compose No. 184, not knowing at the time that the task had already been achieved by the New England composer, Walter I. Kennard (*1860–1936*). Mr. Kennard's position is reproduced in the Appendix as A15.

Several of the illustrative problems already given, especially those illustrating the anti-Bristol, Plachutta and Holzhausen themes, show examples of the decoy of black pieces. Problem 185 illustrates the *Roman theme,* which is a specialized form of decoy of black. Weenink in *The Chess Problem* describes a Roman decoy thus: "The distinction between an ordinary decoy and a Roman is as follows: In an ordinary decoy of a black piece away from

181

The Pittsburgh Post
June 6, 1926

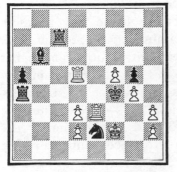

White mates in two moves

182

The Pittsburgh Post
September 26, 1926

White mates in three moves

183

The Pittsburgh Post
October 10, 1926

White mates in four moves

184

American Chess Bulletin
February, 1926

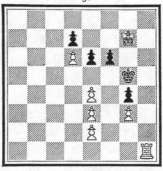

White mates in four moves

a square, the decoyed piece cannot prevent any longer a threat of white, which it could prevent in the initial position. In a Roman decoy the decoyed piece can still defend against an initial try in an analogous way, but such a defence develops a weakening of the black position that would not have developed before the decoy."

This explanation of the Roman theme may be more readily understood by an examination of problem 185. White might play 1 Rf8xP, threatening 2 Rf6 – f4 mate, but black has an adequate defense in 1 — — Rd6, pinning the white rook. Accordingly white first plays 1 Rf7, threatening 2 Re7 mate. If black replies 1 — — Re8, white now captures the pawn, 2 Rf7xPf6, and black's pinning defense, 2 — — Re6, is inadequate since white can play 3 RxR mate.

In the next two positions the white pawns play a leading part, since supported by the rooks they deliver the thematic mates. It is compositions of this type that show some of the most interesting possibilities of rook and pawn play. The capture key in No. 186, 1 PxP, can hardly be regarded as a defect, because from first appearances it would seem that during the course of the solution the capture of the black pawn would have to be made by one of the rooks, and the capture by the white pawn apparently blocks the rooks' action. The problem shows chameleon echoed model mates by a pawn with rook support. The thematic variations run: 1 PxP, Pg5; 2 Rh3 ck, Ke4; 3 Rf3, Pg4; 4 Pd3, and 1 — — Kc4; 2 Pd5 ck, Kc5; 3 Rb4, Pg5; 4 Pd4. Note that the rook's support of the pawn is a lateral one, similar to that in problem 114.

Problem 187 has a greater strategic content, since in each of the thematic lines white makes a clearance for the pawn and induces a black self-block by a rook sacrifice. The key, 1 Ra8 – b8, threatens mate on the next move by

185

The Pittsburgh Post
February 27, 1927

White mates in three moves

186

The Weekly Westminster
August 14, 1926

White mates in four moves

187

The Pittsburgh Post
September 19, 1926

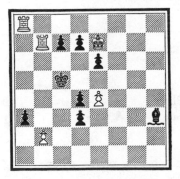

White mates in five moves

188

First Honorable Mention
Twelfth Informal Tourney
The Weekly Westminster
January 16, 1926

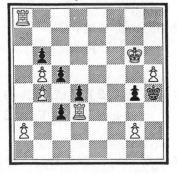

White mates in four moves

2 RxP. This is termed a *short threat,* i. e., a threatened mate in less than the number of moves required by the conditions of the problem. This is an undesirable feature, but it is not considered so objectionable in a problem of this type, which is composed to show an elaborate echo, as it would be in an ordinary three-mover. In this problem, like the preceding one, there are chameleon model mates delivered by a white pawn.

No. 188 is a rook and pawn problem with four full length continuations, three of which end in model mates and the fourth in a pin-mate. The problem is of the waiting move type; the initial position is an incomplete block, and additional waiting move positions occur throughout the solution. In the various lines of play there is but one checking move by white, a rook sacrifice. Were the author obliged to select only one problem as his favorite composition from the thousand odd that he has composed, this probably would be the one he ultimately would choose.

SOLUTIONS

NO.181
1 Pf6, Rc5; 2 Rf3
　　Sd4; 2 Re4

NO.182
1 Ra3, Pa5; 2 Rg3 ck, PxR; *3* Ph4
　　　　Pf4; 2 Rc5 ck, Kg4; *3* Ph3

NO.183
1 Rg6, PxR; 2 KxS, Pg5;　　　*3* Kf6, Pg4;　*4* PxP
　　　Se8; 2 KxP, Sf6 ck;　　　*3* PxS, Pe5;　*4* RxP
　　　Sf5; 2 Rg1–g5 ck, PxRg5;　*3* KxP, Pg4;　*4* PxP
　　　　　　　　　　　　　　　　　　S any;　*4* Rh6

NO.184
1 Rel, Pf5; *2* Pe5, Pf4; *3* Pe3xP ck, Kf5; *4* Pe4

NO.185
1 Rf7, Re8; *2* Rf7xPf6
    Rd7; *2* RxR

NO.186
1 PxP, Pg5; *2* Rh3 ck, Ke4; *3* Rf3, Pg4; *4* Pd3
    Kc4; *2* Pd5 ck, Kc5; *3* Rb4, Pg5; *4* Pd4

NO.187
1 Ra8–b8, Pc6; *2* Pb3, Pa2; *3* Rb4, Pd5; *4* Rc4 ck, PxR; *5* Pb4
      Kc6; *2* Pb4, Bg2; *3* Rb5, Pd6; *4* Rc5 ck, PxR; *5* Pb5

NO.188
1 Ra3, PxP; *2* Rb3, Pc2;   *3* RxQP, Pc1;   *4* Rh3
    Pc2; *2* Kf5, KxP;   *3* Rh3 ck, PxR; *4* RxP
    Pc4; *2* QRxP, Px(either)R; *3* RxP, Pg3;   *4* RxPc4(d4)
    Pg3; *2* Re3, PxR;   *3* RxP, Kg4;   *4* Rc4

17

Self–Mates

THE SELF-MATE problem boasts of nearly as honorable an antiquity as the direct-mate. The older self-mates, like the direct-mates of the past, usually had only a single line of play and frequently were of inordinate length, and although the multi-variation direct-mate began to be developed over two generations ago, it was some time later before composers started to produce self-mates with much choice or variety in the lines of defense.

Similarly to the direct-mate problem, the introduction of variations in the self-mate has gone hand in hand with the shortening of the number of moves required for the solution. It is well within a century, however, that it has come to be recognized generally that there are plenty of ideas which can be expressed in self-mate form in three-move or even two-move settings. Now it has been discovered that the self-mate is often peculiarly adapted for the illustration of many ideas that are difficult, if not impossible, to show in direct-mate settings. Dr. Bettmann's "Babsontask" problem, given in the Appendix, is a typical example. In other cases where a theme has been shown so frequently in direct-mate settings that the possibilities for any new effects in that form have become exhausted,

189

First Prize
Second Quarter, 1931
Die Schwalbe

White self-mates in two moves

190

Solving Contest
Marshall Chess Club
House Opening
December 19, 1931

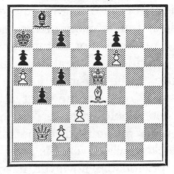

White self-mates in two moves

191

Globo (Rio de Janeiro)
October 5, 1931

White self-mates in two moves

192

Skakbladet
May, 1931

White self-mates in two moves

the self-mate sometimes affords opportunities for further novelty in its illustration.

For a self-mate to be accurately constructed white should have no dual continuations. On the other hand, not only a choice of defenses by black but also a choice of mating moves, is not considered a defect but rather a merit, because it gives increased variety to the play. In the self-mate many of the requisites of good construction are reversed. For instance, whereas in the direct-mate it is considered desirable to have mates of the black king pure, in the self-mate field it is the white king's field that usually receives the most attention, although some composers would go a step further and strive to have all the squares in the fields of both kings only singly guarded or blocked, whenever it is possible to do so. This would only be practicable, however, in longer problems as a rule, and for that matter too great attention to purity of mating positions is no more compatible with highly strategic problems in self-mate settings than it is in direct-mates. In problem 190, however, the white king's field is arranged so that all the mates are pure and the squares in the black king's field are only singly guarded or blocked in two of the lines of play. This was easy to do in the case of the white king since all of the mates are actually given by the unmasked bishop.

The first illustrative problem in this chapter, No. 189, was specifically composed to show a self-mate similar to a multi-variation direct-mate two-mover. This is a threat problem, with five variations, making six lines of play altogether, as follows: 1 Qb4, threat 2 Qd2 ck, KxQ. 1 — — Qa5; 2 Qe1 ck, QxQ. 1 — — Qf6 ck; 2 Sf2 ck, QxS. 1 — — Qg5; 2 BxR ck, BxB. 1 — — BxB; 2 Qe1 ck, RxQ. 1 — — Sf3; 2 Sf2 ck, RxS. There is no thematic relation between the mates and it will be found that the self-mate lends itself better to more closely knit thematic renderings such as are shown in the succeeding positions.

In No. 190 black's queen's bishop's pawn is forced to three different squares to discover mate from the bishop. Note that this is an incomplete block position and that white can not advance the pawn two squares immediately because he needs to make a waiting move again with the pawn when black plays 1 — — Pb3. Incidentally the keymove introduces an additional variation. In No. 191 and No. 192 the rook and the bishop respectively are forced to play to five squares each to discover mate. In neither case is this anywhere nearly the maximum number of squares possible, but similarly to direct-mate composition more artistic results often can be obtained when the composer does not strive to attain task records.

In Chapter Twelve problems 125 and 126 illustrated how certain strategic themes can be presented both in diagonal and orthogonal settings. In fact, in connection with No. 122 it was pointed out that the idea of the composition was a diagonal adaptation of a theme that had been originally shown in orthogonal form by Hume and Pirnie. Problems 191 and 192 are additional examples, in self-mate dress, of the illustration of the same idea diagonally and orthogonally.

Hume published a white half-pin self-mate in the *Chess Amateur* in November, 1921, upon which Alain C. White commented in *Changing Fashions*: "Theoretically the white half-pin should be the standard in the self-mate, where it is customary to find direct mate strategical forms inverted as to the colors used; but so far as there have been experiments made to date . . . there is little to indicate that the white half-pin will lead to any extensive body of new problem possibilities." One reason for this is undoubtedly due to the fact that in self-mates the fields of both kings have to be guarded, instead of only the black king's field as in the case of the direct-mate. This often involves the use of so many men for purely guarding purposes that there are not sufficient men remaining for elaborate strategic combinations.

In addition to Hume's white half-pin self-mate the author had seen a few others, and these problems led him to make a series of experiments in this field, five examples of which are reproduced in this chapter. Unlike the black half-pin, with which it is easy to combine many other strategic elements, the thematic content of these positions will be found to be rather closely limited to the purely half-pin play.

Problem 193 shows a lateral half-pin of the white queen and rook with four half-pin variations. In No. 194 the threat leads to a half-pin mate and there are three additional thematic variations. This problem has a mildly strategic elaboration in the two interferences by the black knight. Problem 195 is a position where black has a choice of mating moves following the threat line, but only one of these results in a half-pin mate. There are two half-pin variations. No. 196 also has a thematic threat and two thematic variations. Finally No. 197 shows an unusual form of half-pin, that of a diagonally pinned queen and bishop. Here the keymove itself is thematic, setting up the half-pin formation, and there are again three thematic lines of play. None of these five positions suggest that there is much probability of increasing the field for white half-pin composition by the combination of other interesting features with the half-pins.

The next position is a black castler in self-mate form with the mates given by discovery by moves of the black bishop. The chief interest in the problem lies in the fact that these mates occur with the black king standing re-

193

Die Schwalbe
July, 1932

White self-mates in two moves

194

Die Schwalbe
September, 1932

White self-mates in two moves

195

Dagens Nyheder
September 30, 1934

White self-mates in two moves

196

Die Schwalbe
May, 1933

White self-mates in two moves

197

British Chess Magazine
December, 1933

White self-mates in two moves

198

First Honorable Mention for
Self-Mates
Second Quarter, 1930
Die Schwalbe

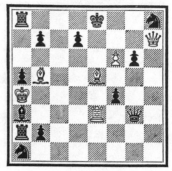

White self-mates in two moves

199

British Chess Magazine
December, 1932

White self-mates in four moves

200

Skakbladet
April, 1930

White self-mates in eight moves

spectively on four different squares, f8, e8, d8 and c8. Problem 199, a white castler, is confessedly a task effort and suffers from a drastic key.

The last diagram, problem 200, illustrates the old one-line style of self-mate composition in modern dress. In the final position the three squares adjacent to each king are singly guarded or blocked. The order of the moves must be made in an accurate sequence and there are switch-backs of two pieces in the course of the solution, which is more whimsical than strategic.

SOLUTIONS

NO.189
1 Qb4

NO.190
1 Pc3, PxP; 2 Qb6 ck
    Pb3; 2 Pc4
    Pd4; 2 Qf2 ck

NO.191
1 Bd4, *threat* 2 Qe5 ck
    KRxP; 2 SxR ck
    BxP; 2 Qf5 ck
    Sd5; 2 PxS ck
    Bc5; 2 SxB ck

NO.192
1 Kh3, *threat* 2 Rg4 ck
    Rg5; 2 Rf3 ck
    QxP; 2 SxQ ck
    Pf5; 2 Sg6 ck
    Se5; 2 QRxP ck

NO.193
1 Sh6, *threat* 2 KSxP ck
    Pf4; 2 Re4 ck
    Qe3, g3; 2 Qe5 ck
    SxS; 2 QxQP ck
    RxS; 2 QxBP ck

NO.194
1 Sf2, *threat* 2 QxPf4 ck
    Se6; 2 QxPf6 ck
    Sd3; 2 Sg3 ck
    RxQ; 2 QRxP ck

NO.195
1 Re3, *threat* 2 RxQP ck
    Qg6, h7; 2 Re4 ck
    Bf1; 2 SxP ck

NO.196
1 Sd7, *threat* 2 Rg6 ck
    QxR; 2 Ph4 ck
    Sf3; 2 Rg4 ck

NO.197   NO.198

1 Kh1, *threat* 2 QxS ck   1 Re4, *threat* 2 Qe7 ck

    Sb2 ck; 2 Qf1 ck   Kf8; 2 Bd6 ck

    SxP ck; 2 Bf1 ck   Kd8; 2 QxS ck

                               0 - 0 - 0; 2 Rc4 ck

                               Sf7; 2 Qg8 ck

NO.199

1 Pf8=S, Pa4; 2 Bd2, Pa3; 3 0 - 0 - 0, Pa2;   4 Qd3 ck, SxQ

         PxB; 2 Ra4, Pf3; 3 0 - 0, PxP;   4 Qf3 ck, SxQ

NO.200

1 Bd3; 2 Sf3; 3 0 - 0; 4 Rd1; 5 Bf1; 6 Kh1; 7 Sg1; 8 Bg2, PxB.

Appendix

PROBLEM A1 was reproduced as No. 100 in Alain C. White's *Running the Gauntlet*, with the comment: "It is . . . the only position I know in which Running the Gauntlet figures as a try. There are many other ways in which it might be used, and I recommend the subject to those who want to compose a puzzling position for a solving tourney." The author remembered this position when he was invited to compose some problems for the Cleveland vs. Cincinnati Solving Contest that was held in 1934 and he accordingly constructed No. 11. In No. A1 the try 1 Pd4 is defeated only by one move, 1 — — Bd8.

No. A2 and No. A3 are the task problems referred to on page 50. It is noteworthy that there are no duals in No. A2. This results from the fact that the mates in the variations are effective only when the square e4 is blocked. No. A3 is a complete block in the initial setting and the keymove changes the mate after 1 — — SxP. It is remarkable to have so fine a key in a record task composition. Ua Tane is a Polynesian name that was given to the American composer James F. Stimson (*b. 1883*), who went to live on the South Sea island of Moörea. A. J. Fink *(1890–1956)* was a Californian composer and player.

The author contributed a two-mover in 1926 to the *Bristol Times and Mirror* that had quadrupled simultaneous unpinning of a laterally pinned black queen and a diagonally pinned white one. One of the variations, however, was thematically imperfect because the unpinned white queen mated without leaving the line of pin. Problem 48, with its tripled simultaneous unpinning of both queens, is an adaptation of the *Bristol Times* problem. Funk's No. A4 shows four thematic unpins, but the black piece that is unpinned is a bishop instead of a queen.

No. A5 was mentioned on page 72 as the earliest known example of a complete half-pin. The key is thematic since it sets up the half-pin, but nowadays the unprovided check in the initial position, 1 — — Rb6 ck, would be considered a serious flaw. An "unprovided flight" was defined in Chapter Four. An *unprovided check* is a check threatened by black in the initial position of a problem for which white has no reply already set that will defend against the check and mate black at the same time (if the problem is a two-mover).

No. A6 has two less white men than No. 54, and, although the key is the same in both problems, it is much more striking in Hesslegren's setting. Furthermore the homogeneous half-pinned pairs in the latter have a more attractive effect than have the heterogeneous pairs in the author's composition.

No. A7 is the classic illustration, referred to on page 74, of the combination of a half-pin with direct checks by both members of the half-pinned pair. The key, 1 Qa1, is doubly thematic in that it both sets up the half-pinning of the black pieces and also makes possible the cross-checks. The first, in itself, might be regarded as restrictive and hence theoretically poor for a keymove even though thematic, but the allowing of the cross-checks more than

A1

L. H. Jokisch
Tidskrift for Schack
1909

White mates in two moves

A2

Murray Marble
First Prize
La Stratégie
1909

White mates in two moves

A3

A. J. Fink and Ua Tane
First Prize
Good Companions
July, 1920

White mates in two moves

A4

Jacob E. Funk
Good Companions
1923

White mates in two moves

counterbalances the restrictive feature of the half-pinning. In this composition note especially that both of the black checks are direct. In most of the limited number of problems that have been composed to show the blend of half-pin and cross-checks, one of the black checks is direct and the other is given by discovery.

The Hume theme derived its name from A8, as mentioned on page 92. The thematic variations run: 1 Sh4 (threat 2 PxP), QSe3; 2 QxKBP. 1 — — KSe3 or b6; 2 QxQP. 1 — — Sc7; 2 RxP.

Traxler's problem, No. A9, has five model mating positions, including the same chameleon echoed pawn mates by the bishop's pawn as in No. 114. On the other hand the latter problem has the echoed rook mates in the secondary lines of play as a distinctive feature. The fundamental distinction between the two compositions, however, is that the queen's pawn is supported by the king in No. A9 and by the rook in No. 114.

The two pairs of problems, No. 122 and No. A10, and No. 131 and No. A11, are typical examples of how the same theme may be illustrated both diagonally and orthogonally. After seeing problem A10, the author set out to construct a position with a check by the black queen on a diagonal line followed by a withdrawal move of the white king leaving the black queen pinned. No. 122 was the result.

Jacobs had seen Ernst's orthogonal rendering, mentioned on page 148, of triple consecutive anticipatory line-closings or shut-offs of black pieces, and proceeded to illustrate the theme diagonally, No. A11, using a white bishop in place of the white rook used by Ernst. No. 131 is a refinement on Ernst's problem.

The waiting move arrangement in No. A12 is actually the simplest manner in which the combined orthogonal

A5

A. Kempe
Cassell's Family Paper
1855

White mates in two moves

A6

A. Hesselgren
Second Prize
Budapest Chess Club
Tourney
1932–1933

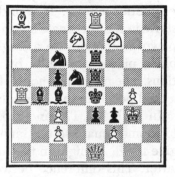

White mates in two moves

A7

Alain White
Good Companions
March, 1920

White mates in two moves

A8

George Hume
Second Prize (ex aequo)
Eighth American Chess
Congress
1921

White mates in two moves

and diagonal Plachuttas can be set, but it lacks the unified construction of No. 136, being more similar to No. 135, in which there is no relation between the two pairs of black interfering pieces.

On page 171 it was mentioned that the self-mate form of problem is peculiarly adapted for showing various pawn promotion effects. It would be practically impossible to show in a direct-mate setting the theme of No. A13, black pawn promotions on a single square to the four kinds of black pieces countered by identical white pawn promotions. The minor promotion for a keymove in No. A13 adds a final polish to this marvellous composition.

In both No. 170 and No. A14 the white king vacates his home square so that another piece may move there to give mate; a knight in the former position, a bishop in the latter. This difference between the mating pieces makes entirely different settings necessary for the two problems.

No. 184 has a more striking key than No. A15, because in the former the rook withdraws from an apparently strong position and also gives the black king a flight square, while in the initial position of No. A15 the rook obviously is out of play. Nevertheless Kennard is entitled to the honor of having first shown the tripled pawn ambush with the rook below the pawns.

Problem A16 is reproduced here to illustrate what is termed *focal play*, since there is no good example of this theme shown elsewhere in the book. According to Weenink the first known example of the theme was in a threemover published by C. Stanley ("of the Brighton Chess Club") in the *Illustrated London News*, October 6, 1849. The theme was largely exploited by Baron von Holzhausen, who dealt with it in articles which appeared in 1908 and 1909 in the *Deutsches Wochenschach*, and later

A9

P. K. Traxler
Šachové Listy
1900

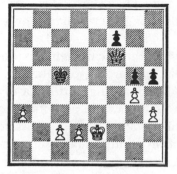

White mates in four moves

A10

George Hume and D. Pirnie
Daily News
September 8, 1923

White mates in three moves

A11

Walter Jacobs
American Chess Bulletin
January, 1936

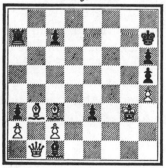

White mates in four moves

A12

V. Kukainis
Second Prize, 1938
Stasti un Romani

White mates in three moves

were expanded into a volume entitled *Brennpunktprobleme*, which was published in 1926.

In the focal theme, a black piece guards two squares, which von Holzhausen called *foci*, and, to quote Weenink, "it is usually possible for the principal black piece, often the Queen, to guard these foci from several squares, and the play consists in obstructing these guards or in otherwise neutralizing them."

In *Simple Two-Move Themes* the focal theme is defined thus: "Where the simple unguarding of squares is repeated in such a way that the guarding and releasing of two definite squares controls the whole activity of a black long-range piece, Queen, Rook or Bishop, and also controls the mating movement of White, usually of a single white piece, the problem is called a Focal problem. The Foci are the guarded squares, and the solution depends on providing mates at the Foci and then forcing Black to surrender one or other of the guards thereat."

Focal play is more commonly found in problems in three or four moves, but it may be shown in a two-mover and the author has selected No. A16 to illustrate the theme, because this problem actually presents the theme in a mutate setting. In the initial position there are two foci, d2 and g3, guarded by the black rook, on one or the other of which white's king's knight can mate if the black rook moves. White, however, has no waiting move. The key, 1 Qa6, changes the foci to e2 and g6; the queen mating on one or the other of these squares according to the black rook's moves.

A 13

Henry Wald Bettmann
First Prize
"Babsontask" Contest
1926

White self-mates in three
moves

A 14

Alain White
Frontispiece
The Properties of Castling
1928

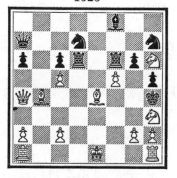

White mates in three moves

A 15

W. I. Kennard
American Chess Bulletin
December, 1915

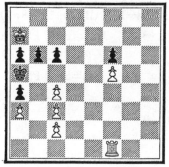

White mates in four moves

A 16

Comins Mansfield
Morning Post
April, 1923

White mates in two moves

SOLUTIONS

NO.A1	NO.A2	NO.A3
1 Pd3	*1* Be4	*1* Rc8

NO.A4	NO.A5	NO.A6
1 Sh8	*1* Rd8	*1* Qe2

NO.A7	NO.A8
1 Qa1	*1* Sh4

NO.A9

1 Qa6, Kd4; 2 Qa5, Ke4; 3 Pd3 ck, Kd4; 4 Pc3
                                      Kf4; 4 Qc7

        Kd5; 2 Ke3, Ke5; 3 Pd4 ck, Kd5; 4 Pc4
                  Pf5; 3 Pc4 ck, Kc5; 4 Pd4

        Pf5; 2 Ke3, Pf4 ck; 3 Ke4, any;   4 Pd4

NO.A10

l Qh5, Qg5 ck; 2 KxP

NO.A11

1 Bf6, Kg6; 2 Be5, Kf5; 3 Bd4, Ke4; 4 Pc3

NO.A12

1 Sg5, Be2; 2 SxQP ck
       Qe2; 2 SxBP ck
       QRg7; 2 Sf7 ck
       KRg7; 2 SxSP ck

NO.A13

1 Pa8=B, PxB=Q; 2 Pf8=Q
           PxB=R; 2 Pf8=R
           PxB=B; 2 Pf8=B
           PxB=S; 2 Pf8=S

NO.A14

1 Bd5, Pg5;   2 O–O–O
       PxPf5 *or* KRe6 ck; 2 Kf1
                   Se5; 2 Ke1
       PxB *or* QRe6 ck; 2 Kd1
                   Sb6; 2 O–O (*threat*).

NO.A15

1 Rc1, Pb5; 2 Pc5, Pb4; *3* BPxP ck

NO.A16

1 Qa6

Index of Individuals

General Index

**A CATALOGUE OF SELECTED DOVER BOOKS
IN ALL FIELDS OF INTEREST**

A CATALOGUE OF SELECTED DOVER
BOOKS IN ALL FIELDS OF INTEREST

RACKHAM'S COLOR ILLUSTRATIONS FOR WAGNER'S RING. Rackham's finest mature work—all 64 full-color watercolors in a faithful and lush interpretation of the *Ring*. Full-sized plates on coated stock of the paintings used by opera companies for authentic staging of Wagner. Captions aid in following complete Ring cycle. Introduction. 64 illustrations plus vignettes. 72pp. 8⅝ x 11¼.   23779-6 Pa. $6.00

CONTEMPORARY POLISH POSTERS IN FULL COLOR, edited by Joseph Czestochowski. 46 full-color examples of brilliant school of Polish graphic design, selected from world's first museum (near Warsaw) dedicated to poster art. Posters on circuses, films, plays, concerts all show cosmopolitan influences, free imagination. Introduction. 48pp. 9⅜ x 12¼.   23780-X Pa. $6.00

GRAPHIC WORKS OF EDVARD MUNCH, Edvard Munch. 90 haunting, evocative prints by first major Expressionist artist and one of the greatest graphic artists of his time: *The Scream, Anxiety, Death Chamber, The Kiss, Madonna,* etc. Introduction by Alfred Werner. 90pp. 9 x 12.   23765-6 Pa. $5.00

THE GOLDEN AGE OF THE POSTER, Hayward and Blanche Cirker. 70 extraordinary posters in full colors, from Maitres de l'Affiche, Mucha, Lautrec, Bradley, Cheret, Beardsley, many others. Total of 78pp. 9⅜ x 12¼.   22753-7 Pa. $5.95

THE NOTEBOOKS OF LEONARDO DA VINCI, edited by J. P. Richter. Extracts from manuscripts reveal great genius; on painting, sculpture, anatomy, sciences, geography, etc. Both Italian and English. 186 ms. pages reproduced, plus 500 additional drawings, including studies for *Last Supper,* Sforza monument, etc. 860pp. 7⅞ x 10¾. (Available in U.S. only)   22572-0, 22573-9 Pa., Two-vol. set $15.90

THE CODEX NUTTALL, as first edited by Zelia Nuttall. Only inexpensive edition, in full color, of a pre-Columbian Mexican (Mixtec) book. 88 color plates show kings, gods, heroes, temples, sacrifices. New explanatory historical introduction by Arthur G. Miller. 96pp. 11⅜ x 8½. (Available in U.S. only)   23168-2 Pa. $7.95

UNE SEMAINE DE BONTÉ, A SURREALISTIC NOVEL IN COLLAGE, Max Ernst. Masterpiece created out of 19th-century periodical illustrations, explores worlds of terror and surprise. Some consider this Ernst's greatest work. 208pp. 8⅛ x 11.   23252-2 Pa. $6.00

UNCLE SILAS, J. Sheridan LeFanu. Victorian Gothic mystery novel, considered by many best of period, even better than Collins or Dickens. Wonderful psychological terror. Introduction by Frederick Shroyer. 436pp. 5⅜ x 8½.   21715-9 Pa. $6.00

JURGEN, James Branch Cabell. The great erotic fantasy of the 1920's that delighted thousands, shocked thousands more. Full final text, Lane edition with 13 plates by Frank Pape. 346pp. 5⅜ x 8½.
23507-6 Pa. $4.50

THE CLAVERINGS, Anthony Trollope. Major novel, chronicling aspects of British Victorian society, personalities. Reprint of Cornhill serialization, 16 plates by M. Edwards; first reprint of full text. Introduction by Norman Donaldson. 412pp. 5⅜ x 8½.   23464-9 Pa. $5.00

KEPT IN THE DARK, Anthony Trollope. Unusual short novel about Victorian morality and abnormal psychology by the great English author. Probably the first American publication. Frontispiece by Sir John Millais. 92pp. 6½ x 9¼.   23609-9 Pa. $2.50

RALPH THE HEIR, Anthony Trollope. Forgotten tale of illegitimacy, inheritance. Master novel of Trollope's later years. Victorian country estates, clubs, Parliament, fox hunting, world of fully realized characters. Reprint of 1871 edition. 12 illustrations by F. A. Faser. 434pp. of text. 5⅜ x 8½.   23642-0 Pa. $5.00

YEKL and THE IMPORTED BRIDEGROOM AND OTHER STORIES OF THE NEW YORK GHETTO, Abraham Cahan. Film *Hester Street* based on *Yekl* (1896). Novel, other stories among first about Jewish immigrants of N.Y.'s East Side. Highly praised by W. D. Howells—Cahan "a new star of realism." New introduction by Bernard G. Richards. 240pp. 5⅜ x 8½.   22427-9 Pa. $3.50

THE HIGH PLACE, James Branch Cabell. Great fantasy writer's enchanting comedy of disenchantment set in 18th-century France. Considered by some critics to be even better than his famous *Jurgen*. 10 illustrations and numerous vignettes by noted fantasy artist Frank C. Pape. 320pp. 5⅜ x 8½.   23670-6 Pa. $4.00

ALICE'S ADVENTURES UNDER GROUND, Lewis Carroll. Facsimile of ms. Carroll gave Alice Liddell in 1864. Different in many ways from final Alice. Handlettered, illustrated by Carroll. Introduction by Martin Gardner. 128pp. 5⅜ x 8½.   21482-6 Pa. $2.50

FAVORITE ANDREW LANG FAIRY TALE BOOKS IN MANY COLORS, Andrew Lang. The four Lang favorites in a boxed set—the complete *Red, Green, Yellow* and *Blue* Fairy Books. 164 stories; 439 illustrations by Lancelot Speed, Henry Ford and G. P. Jacomb Hood. Total of about 1500pp. 5⅜ x 8½.   23407-X Boxed set, Pa. $15.95

A MAYA GRAMMAR, Alfred M. Tozzer. Practical, useful English-language grammar by the Harvard anthropologist who was one of the three greatest American scholars in the area of Maya culture. Phonetics, grammatical processes, syntax, more. 301pp. 5⅜ x 8½. 23465-7 Pa. $4.00

THE JOURNAL OF HENRY D. THOREAU, edited by Bradford Torrey, F. H. Allen. Complete reprinting of 14 volumes, 1837-61, over two million words; the sourcebooks for *Walden*, etc. Definitive. All original sketches, plus 75 photographs. Introduction by Walter Harding. Total of 1804pp. 8½ x 12¼. 20312-3, 20313-1 Clothbd., Two-vol. set $70.00

CLASSIC GHOST STORIES, Charles Dickens and others. 18 wonderful stories you've wanted to reread: "The Monkey's Paw," "The House and the Brain," "The Upper Berth," "The Signalman," "Dracula's Guest," "The Tapestried Chamber," etc. Dickens, Scott, Mary Shelley, Stoker, etc. 330pp. 5⅜ x 8½. 20735-8 Pa. $4.50

SEVEN SCIENCE FICTION NOVELS, H. G. Wells. Full novels. *First Men in the Moon, Island of Dr. Moreau, War of the Worlds, Food of the Gods, Invisible Man, Time Machine, In the Days of the Comet.* A basic science-fiction library. 1015pp. 5⅜ x 8½. (Available in U.S. only) 20264-X Clothbd. $8.95

ARMADALE, Wilkie Collins. Third great mystery novel by the author of *The Woman in White* and *The Moonstone*. Ingeniously plotted narrative shows an exceptional command of character, incident and mood. Original magazine version with 40 illustrations. 597pp. 5⅜ x 8½. 23429-0 Pa. $6.00

MASTERS OF MYSTERY, H. Douglas Thomson. The first book in English (1931) devoted to history and aesthetics of detective story. Poe, Doyle, LeFanu, Dickens, many others, up to 1930. New introduction and notes by E. F. Bleiler. 288pp. 5⅜ x 8½. (Available in U.S. only) 23606-4 Pa. $4.00

FLATLAND, E. A. Abbott. Science-fiction classic explores life of 2-D being in 3-D world. Read also as introduction to thought about hyperspace. Introduction by Banesh Hoffmann. 16 illustrations. 103pp. 5⅜ x 8½. 20001-9 Pa. $2.00

THREE SUPERNATURAL NOVELS OF THE VICTORIAN PERIOD, edited, with an introduction, by E. F. Bleiler. Reprinted complete and unabridged, three great classics of the supernatural: *The Haunted Hotel* by Wilkie Collins, *The Haunted House at Latchford* by Mrs. J. H. Riddell, and *The Lost Stradivarius* by J. Meade Falkner. 325pp. 5⅜ x 8½. 22571-2 Pa. $4.00

AYESHA: THE RETURN OF "SHE," H. Rider Haggard. Virtuoso sequel featuring the great mythic creation, Ayesha, in an adventure that is fully as good as the first book, *She*. Original magazine version, with 47 original illustrations by Maurice Greiffenhagen. 189pp. 6½ x 9¼. 23649-8 Pa. $3.50

PRINCIPLES OF ORCHESTRATION, Nikolay Rimsky-Korsakov. Great classical orchestrator provides fundamentals of tonal resonance, progression of parts, voice and orchestra, tutti effects, much else in major document. 330pp. of musical excerpts. 489pp. 6½ x 9¼. 21266-1 Pa. $7.50

TRISTAN UND ISOLDE, Richard Wagner. Full orchestral score with complete instrumentation. Do not confuse with piano reduction. Commentary by Felix Mottl, great Wagnerian conductor and scholar. Study score. 655pp. 8⅛ x 11. 22915-7 Pa. $13.95

REQUIEM IN FULL SCORE, Giuseppe Verdi. Immensely popular with choral groups and music lovers. Republication of edition published by C. F. Peters, Leipzig, n. d. German frontmaker in English translation. Glossary. Text in Latin. Study score. 204pp. 9⅜ x 12¼. 23682-X Pa. $6.00

COMPLETE CHAMBER MUSIC FOR STRINGS, Felix Mendelssohn. All of Mendelssohn's chamber music: Octet, 2 Quintets, 6 Quartets, and Four Pieces for String Quartet. (Nothing with piano is included). Complete works edition (1874-7). Study score. 283 pp. 9⅜ x 12¼. 23679-X Pa. $7.50

POPULAR SONGS OF NINETEENTH-CENTURY AMERICA, edited by Richard Jackson. 64 most important songs: "Old Oaken Bucket," "Arkansas Traveler," "Yellow Rose of Texas," etc. Authentic original sheet music, full introduction and commentaries. 290pp. 9 x 12. 23270-0 Pa. $7.95

COLLECTED PIANO WORKS, Scott Joplin. Edited by Vera Brodsky Lawrence. Practically all of Joplin's piano works—rags, two-steps, marches, waltzes, etc., 51 works in all. Extensive Introduction by Rudi Blesh. Total of 345pp. 9 x 12. 23106-2 Pa. $14.95

BASIC PRINCIPLES OF CLASSICAL BALLET, Agrippina Vaganova. Great Russian theoretician, teacher explains methods for teaching classical ballet; incorporates best from French, Italian, Russian schools. 118 illustrations. 175pp. 5⅜ x 8½. 22036-2 Pa. $2.50

CHINESE CHARACTERS, L. Wieger. Rich analysis of 2300 characters according to traditional systems into primitives. Historical-semantic analysis to phonetics (Classical Mandarin) and radicals. 820pp. 6⅛ x 9¼. 21321-8 Pa. $10.00

EGYPTIAN LANGUAGE: EASY LESSONS IN EGYPTIAN HIEROGLYPHICS, E. A. Wallis Budge. Foremost Egyptologist offers Egyptian grammar, explanation of hieroglyphics, many reading texts, dictionary of symbols. 246pp. 5 x 7½. (Available in U.S. only) 21394-3 Clothbd. $7.50

AN ETYMOLOGICAL DICTIONARY OF MODERN ENGLISH, Ernest Weekley. Richest, fullest work, by foremost British lexicographer. Detailed word histories. Inexhaustible. Do not confuse this with Concise Etymological Dictionary, which is abridged. Total of 856pp. 6½ x 9¼. 21873-2, 21874-0 Pa.; Two-vol. set $12.00

HOLLYWOOD GLAMOUR PORTRAITS, edited by John Kobal. 145 photos capture the stars from 1926-49, the high point in portrait photography. Gable, Harlow, Bogart, Bacall, Hedy Lamarr, Marlene Dietrich, Robert Montgomery, Marlon Brando, Veronica Lake; 94 stars in all. Full background on photographers, technical aspects, much more. Total of 160pp. 8⅜ x 11¼. 23352-9 Pa. $6.00

THE NEW YORK STAGE: FAMOUS PRODUCTIONS IN PHOTOGRAPHS, edited by Stanley Appelbaum. 148 photographs from Museum of City of New York show 142 plays, 1883-1939. *Peter Pan, The Front Page, Dead End, Our Town,* O'Neill, hundreds of actors and actresses, etc. Full indexes. 154pp. 9½ x 10. 23241-7 Pa. $6.00

DIALOGUES CONCERNING TWO NEW SCIENCES, Galileo Galilei. Encompassing 30 years of experiment and thought, these dialogues deal with geometric demonstrations of fracture of solid bodies, cohesion, leverage, speed of light and sound, pendulums, falling bodies, accelerated motion, etc. 300pp. 5⅜ x 8½. 60099-8 Pa. $4.00

THE GREAT OPERA STARS IN HISTORIC PHOTOGRAPHS, edited by James Camner. 343 portraits from the 1850s to the 1940s: Tamburini, Mario, Caliapin, Jeritza, Melchior, Melba, Patti, Pinza, Schipa, Caruso, Farrar, Steber, Gobbi, and many more—270 performers in all. Index. 199pp. 8⅜ x 11¼. 23575-0 Pa. $7.50

J. S. BACH, Albert Schweitzer. Great full-length study of Bach, life, background to music, music, by foremost modern scholar. Ernest Newman translation. 650 musical examples. Total of 928pp. 5⅜ x 8½. (Available in U.S. only) 21631-4, 21632-2 Pa., Two-vol. set $11.00

COMPLETE PIANO SONATAS, Ludwig van Beethoven. All sonatas in the fine Schenker edition, with fingering, analytical material. One of best modern editions. Total of 615pp. 9 x 12. (Available in U.S. only) 23134-8, 23135-6 Pa., Two-vol. set $15.50

KEYBOARD MUSIC, J. S. Bach. Bach-Gesellschaft edition. For harpsichord, piano, other keyboard instruments. English Suites, French Suites, Six Partitas, Goldberg Variations, Two-Part Inventions, Three-Part Sinfonias. 312pp. 8⅛ x 11. (Available in U.S. only) 22360-4 Pa. $6.95

FOUR SYMPHONIES IN FULL SCORE, Franz Schubert. Schubert's four most popular symphonies: No. 4 in C Minor ("Tragic"); No. 5 in B-flat Major; No. 8 in B Minor ("Unfinished"); No. 9 in C Major ("Great"). Breitkopf & Hartel edition. Study score. 261pp. 9⅜ x 12¼. 23681-1 Pa. $6.50

THE AUTHENTIC GILBERT & SULLIVAN SONGBOOK, W. S. Gilbert, A. S. Sullivan. Largest selection available; 92 songs, uncut, original keys, in piano rendering approved by Sullivan. Favorites and lesser-known fine numbers. Edited with plot synopses by James Spero. 3 illustrations. 399pp. 9 x 12. 23482-7 Pa. $9.95

THE DEPRESSION YEARS AS PHOTOGRAPHED BY ARTHUR ROTH-STEIN, Arthur Rothstein. First collection devoted entirely to the work of outstanding 1930s photographer: famous dust storm photo, ragged children, unemployed, etc. 120 photographs. Captions. 119pp. 9¼ x 10¾.
23590-4 Pa. $5.00

CAMERA WORK: A PICTORIAL GUIDE, Alfred Stieglitz. All 559 illustrations and plates from the most important periodical in the history of art photography, Camera Work (1903-17). Presented four to a page, reduced in size but still clear, in strict chronological order, with complete captions. Three indexes. Glossary. Bibliography. 176pp. 8⅜ x 11¼.
23591-2 Pa. $6.95

ALVIN LANGDON COBURN, PHOTOGRAPHER, Alvin L. Coburn. Revealing autobiography by one of greatest photographers of 20th century gives insider's version of Photo-Secession, plus comments on his own work. 77 photographs by Coburn. Edited by Helmut and Alison Gernsheim. 160pp. 8⅛ x 11.
23685-4 Pa. $6.00

NEW YORK IN THE FORTIES, Andreas Feininger. 162 brilliant photographs by the well-known photographer, formerly with Life magazine, show commuters, shoppers, Times Square at night, Harlem nightclub, Lower East Side, etc. Introduction and full captions by John von Hartz. 181pp. 9¼ x 10¾.
23585-8 Pa. $6.95

GREAT NEWS PHOTOS AND THE STORIES BEHIND THEM, John Faber. Dramatic volume of 140 great news photos, 1855 through 1976, and revealing stories behind them, with both historical and technical information. Hindenburg disaster, shooting of Oswald, nomination of Jimmy Carter, etc. 160pp. 8¼ x 11.
23667-6 Pa. $5.00

THE ART OF THE CINEMATOGRAPHER, Leonard Maltin. Survey of American cinematography history and anecdotal interviews with 5 masters—Arthur Miller, Hal Mohr, Hal Rosson, Lucien Ballard, and Conrad Hall. Very large selection of behind-the-scenes production photos. 105 photographs. Filmographies. Index. Originally Behind the Camera. 144pp. 8¼ x 11.
23686-2 Pa. $5.00

DESIGNS FOR THE THREE-CORNERED HAT (LE TRICORNE), Pablo Picasso. 32 fabulously rare drawings—including 31 color illustrations of costumes and accessories—for 1919 production of famous ballet. Edited by Parmenia Migel, who has written new introduction. 48pp. 9⅜ x 12¼. (Available in U.S. only)
23709-5 Pa. $5.00

NOTES OF A FILM DIRECTOR, Sergei Eisenstein. Greatest Russian filmmaker explains montage, making of Alexander Nevsky, aesthetics; comments on self, associates, great rivals (Chaplin), similar material. 78 illustrations. 240pp. 5⅜ x 8½.
22392-2 Pa. $4.50

ART FORMS IN NATURE, Ernst Haeckel. Multitude of strangely beautiful natural forms: Radiolaria, Foraminifera, jellyfishes, fungi, turtles, bats, etc. All 100 plates of the 19th-century evolutionist's *Kunstformen der Natur* (1904). 100pp. 9⅜ x 12¼. 22987-4 Pa. $5.00

CHILDREN: A PICTORIAL ARCHIVE FROM NINETEENTH-CENTURY SOURCES, edited by Carol Belanger Grafton. 242 rare, copyright-free wood engravings for artists and designers. Widest such selection available. All illustrations in line. 119pp. 8⅜ x 11¼. 23694-3 Pa. $4.00

WOMEN: A PICTORIAL ARCHIVE FROM NINETEENTH-CENTURY SOURCES, edited by Jim Harter. 391 copyright-free wood engravings for artists and designers selected from rare periodicals. Most extensive such collection available. All illustrations in line. 128pp. 9 x 12. 23703-6 Pa. $4.50

ARABIC ART IN COLOR, Prisse d'Avennes. From the greatest ornamentalists of all time—50 plates in color, rarely seen outside the Near East, rich in suggestion and stimulus. Includes 4 plates on covers. 46pp. 9⅜ x 12¼. 23658-7 Pa. $6.00

AUTHENTIC ALGERIAN CARPET DESIGNS AND MOTIFS, edited by June Beveridge. Algerian carpets are world famous. Dozens of geometrical motifs are charted on grids, color-coded, for weavers, needleworkers, craftsmen, designers. 53 illustrations plus 4 in color. 48pp. 8¼ x 11. (Available in U.S. only) 23650-1 Pa. $1.75

DICTIONARY OF AMERICAN PORTRAITS, edited by Hayward and Blanche Cirker. 4000 important Americans, earliest times to 1905, mostly in clear line. Politicians, writers, soldiers, scientists, inventors, industrialists, Indians, Blacks, women, outlaws, etc. Identificatory information. 756pp. 9¼ x 12¾. 21823-6 Clothbd. $40.00

HOW THE OTHER HALF LIVES, Jacob A. Riis. Journalistic record of filth, degradation, upward drive in New York immigrant slums, shops, around 1900. New edition includes 100 original Riis photos, monuments of early photography. 233pp. 10 x 7⅞. 22012-5 Pa. $7.00

NEW YORK IN THE THIRTIES, Berenice Abbott. Noted photographer's fascinating study of city shows new buildings that have become famous and old sights that have disappeared forever. Insightful commentary. 97 photographs. 97pp. 11⅜ x 10. 22967-X Pa. $5.00

MEN AT WORK, Lewis W. Hine. Famous photographic studies of construction workers, railroad men, factory workers and coal miners. New supplement of 18 photos on Empire State building construction. New introduction by Jonathan L. Doherty. Total of 69 photos. 63pp. 8 x 10¾. 23475-4 Pa. $3.00

THE ANATOMY OF THE HORSE, George Stubbs. Often considered the great masterpiece of animal anatomy. Full reproduction of 1766 edition, plus prospectus; original text and modernized text. 36 plates. Introduction by Eleanor Garvey. 121pp. 11 x 14¾. 23402-9 Pa. $6.00

BRIDGMAN'S LIFE DRAWING, George B. Bridgman. More than 500 illustrative drawings and text teach you to abstract the body into its major masses, use light and shade, proportion; as well as specific areas of anatomy, of which Bridgman is master. 192pp. 6½ x 9¼. (Available in U.S. only) 22710-3 Pa. $3.50

ART NOUVEAU DESIGNS IN COLOR, Alphonse Mucha, Maurice Verneuil, Georges Auriol. Full-color reproduction of *Combinaisons ornementales* (c. 1900) by Art Nouveau masters. Floral, animal, geometric, interlacings, swashes—borders, frames, spots—all incredibly beautiful. 60 plates, hundreds of designs. 9⅜ x 8-1/16. 22885-1 Pa. $4.00

FULL-COLOR FLORAL DESIGNS IN THE ART NOUVEAU STYLE, E. A. Seguy. 166 motifs, on 40 plates, from *Les fleurs et leurs applications decoratives* (1902): borders, circular designs, repeats, allovers, "spots." All in authentic Art Nouveau colors. 48pp. 9⅜ x 12¼.
23439-8 Pa. $5.00

A DIDEROT PICTORIAL ENCYCLOPEDIA OF TRADES AND IN-DUSTRY, edited by Charles C. Gillispie. 485 most interesting plates from the great French Encyclopedia of the 18th century show hundreds of working figures, artifacts, process, land and cityscapes; glassmaking, papermaking, metal extraction, construction, weaving, making furniture, clothing, wigs, dozens of other activities. Plates fully explained. 920pp. 9 x 12. 22284-5, 22285-3 Clothbd., Two-vol. set $40.00

HANDBOOK OF EARLY ADVERTISING ART, Clarence P. Hornung. Largest collection of copyright-free early and antique advertising art ever compiled. Over 6,000 illustrations, from Franklin's time to the 1890's for special effects, novelty. Valuable source, almost inexhaustible.
Pictorial Volume. Agriculture, the zodiac, animals, autos, birds, Christmas, fire engines, flowers, trees, musical instruments, ships, games and sports, much more. Arranged by subject matter and use. 237 plates. 288pp. 9 x 12.
20122-8 Clothbd. $14.50

Typographical Volume. Roman and Gothic faces ranging from 10 point to 300 point, "Barnum," German and Old English faces, script, logotypes, scrolls and flourishes, 1115 ornamental initials, 67 complete alphabets, more. 310 plates. 320pp. 9 x 12. 20123-6 Clothbd. $15.00

CALLIGRAPHY (CALLIGRAPHIA LATINA), J. G. Schwandner. High point of 18th-century ornamental calligraphy. Very ornate initials, scrolls, borders, cherubs, birds, lettered examples. 172pp. 9 x 13.
20475-8 Pa. $7.00

THE COMPLETE WOODCUTS OF ALBRECHT DURER, edited by Dr. W. Kurth. 346 in all: "Old Testament," "St. Jerome," "Passion," "Life of Virgin," Apocalypse," many others. Introduction by Campbell Dodgson. 285pp. 8½ x 12¼. 21097-9 Pa. $7.50

DRAWINGS OF ALBRECHT DURER, edited by Heinrich Wolfflin. 81 plates show development from youth to full style. Many favorites; many new. Introduction by Alfred Werner. 96pp. 8⅛ x 11. 22352-3 Pa. $5.00

THE HUMAN FIGURE, Albrecht Dürer. Experiments in various techniques—stereometric, progressive proportional, and others. Also life studies that rank among finest ever done. Complete reprinting of *Dresden Sketchbook*. 170 plates. 355pp. 8⅜ x 11¼. 21042-1 Pa. $7.95

OF THE JUST SHAPING OF LETTERS, Albrecht Dürer. Renaissance artist explains design of Roman majuscules by geometry, also Gothic lower and capitals. Grolier Club edition. 43pp. 7⅞ x 10¾ 21306-4 Pa. $3.00

TEN BOOKS ON ARCHITECTURE, Vitruvius. The most important book ever written on architecture. Early Roman aesthetics, technology, classical orders, site selection, all other aspects. Stands behind everything since. Morgan translation. 331pp. 5⅜ x 8½. 20645-9 Pa. $4.50

THE FOUR BOOKS OF ARCHITECTURE, Andrea Palladio. 16th-century classic responsible for Palladian movement and style. Covers classical architectural remains, Renaissance revivals, classical orders, etc. 1738 Ware English edition. Introduction by A. Placzek. 216 plates. 110pp. of text. 9½ x 12¾. 21308-0 Pa. $10.00

HORIZONS, Norman Bel Geddes. Great industrialist stage designer, "father of streamlining," on application of aesthetics to transportation, amusement, architecture, etc. 1932 prophetic account; function, theory, specific projects. 222 illustrations. 312pp. 7⅞ x 10¾. 23514-9 Pa. $6.95

FRANK LLOYD WRIGHT'S FALLINGWATER, Donald Hoffmann. Full, illustrated story of conception and building of Wright's masterwork at Bear Run, Pa. 100 photographs of site, construction, and details of completed structure. 112pp. 9¼ x 10. 23671-4 Pa. $5.50

THE ELEMENTS OF DRAWING, John Ruskin. Timeless classic by great Viltorian; starts with basic ideas, works through more difficult. Many practical exercises. 48 illustrations. Introduction by Lawrence Campbell. 228pp. 5⅜ x 8½. 22730-8 Pa. $3.75

GIST OF ART, John Sloan. Greatest modern American teacher, Art Students League, offers innumerable hints, instructions, guided comments to help you in painting. Not a formal course. 46 illustrations. Introduction by Helen Sloan. 200pp. 5⅜ x 8½. 23435-5 Pa. $4.00

THE EARLY WORK OF AUBREY BEARDSLEY, Aubrey Beardsley. 157 plates, 2 in color: *Manon Lescaut, Madame Bovary, Morte Darthur, Salome,* other. Introduction by H. Marillier. 182pp. 8⅛ x 11. 21816-3 Pa. $4.50

THE LATER WORK OF AUBREY BEARDSLEY, Aubrey Beardsley. Exotic masterpieces of full maturity: *Venus and Tannhauser, Lysistrata, Rape of the Lock, Volpone,* Savoy material, etc. 174 plates, 2 in color. 186pp. 8⅛ x 11. 21817-1 Pa. $5.95

THOMAS NAST'S CHRISTMAS DRAWINGS, Thomas Nast. Almost all Christmas drawings by creator of image of Santa Claus as we know it, and one of America's foremost illustrators and political cartoonists. 66 illustrations. 3 illustrations in color on covers. 96pp. 8⅜ x 11¼. 23660-9 Pa. $3.50

THE DORÉ ILLUSTRATIONS FOR DANTE'S DIVINE COMEDY, Gustave Doré. All 135 plates from Inferno, Purgatory, Paradise; fantastic tortures, infernal landscapes, celestial wonders. Each plate with appropriate (translated) verses. 141pp. 9 x 12. 23231-X Pa. $4.50

DORÉ'S ILLUSTRATIONS FOR RABELAIS, Gustave Doré. 252 striking illustrations of *Gargantua and Pantagruel* books by foremost 19th-century illustrator. Including 60 plates, 192 delightful smaller illustrations. 153pp. 9 x 12. 23656-0 Pa. $5.00

LONDON: A PILGRIMAGE, Gustave Doré, Blanchard Jerrold. Squalor, riches, misery, beauty of mid-Victorian metropolis; 55 wonderful plates, 125 other illustrations, full social, cultural text by Jerrold. 191pp. of text. 9⅜ x 12¼. 22306-X Pa. $7.00

THE RIME OF THE ANCIENT MARINER, Gustave Doré, S. T. Coleridge. Dore's finest work, 34 plates capture moods, subtleties of poem. Full text. Introduction by Millicent Rose. 77pp. 9¼ x 12. 22305-1 Pa. $3.50

THE DORE BIBLE ILLUSTRATIONS, Gustave Doré. All wonderful, detailed plates: Adam and Eve, Flood, Babylon, Life of Jesus, etc. Brief King James text with each plate. Introduction by Millicent Rose. 241 plates. 241pp. 9 x 12. 23004-X Pa. $6.00

THE COMPLETE ENGRAVINGS, ETCHINGS AND DRYPOINTS OF ALBRECHT DURER. "Knight, Death and Devil"; "Melencolia," and more—all Dürer's known works in all three media, including 6 works formerly attributed to him. 120 plates. 235pp. 8⅜ x 11¼. 22851-7 Pa. $6.50

MECHANICK EXERCISES ON THE WHOLE ART OF PRINTING, Joseph Moxon. First complete book (1683-4) ever written about typography, a compendium of everything known about printing at the latter part of 17th century. Reprint of 2nd (1962) Oxford Univ. Press edition. 74 illustrations. Total of 550pp. 6⅛ x 9¼. 23617-X Pa. $7.95

YUCATAN BEFORE AND AFTER THE CONQUEST, Diego de Landa. First English translation of basic book in Maya studies, the only significant account of Yucatan written in the early post-Conquest era. Translated by distinguished Maya scholar William Gates. Appendices, introduction, 4 maps and over 120 illustrations added by translator. 162pp. 5⅜ x 8½.
23622-6 Pa. $3.00

THE MALAY ARCHIPELAGO, Alfred R. Wallace. Spirited travel account by one of founders of modern biology. Touches on zoology, botany, ethnography, geography, and geology. 62 illustrations, maps. 515pp. 5⅜ x 8½.
20187-2 Pa. $6.95

THE DISCOVERY OF THE TOMB OF TUTANKHAMEN, Howard Carter, A. C. Mace. Accompany Carter in the thrill of discovery, as ruined passage suddenly reveals unique, untouched, fabulously rich tomb. Fascinating account, with 106 illustrations. New introduction by J. M. White. Total of 382pp. 5⅜ x 8½. (Available in U.S. only) 23500-9 Pa. $4.00

THE WORLD'S GREATEST SPEECHES, edited by Lewis Copeland and Lawrence W. Lamm. Vast collection of 278 speeches from Greeks up to present. Powerful and effective models; unique look at history. Revised to 1970. Indices. 842pp. 5⅜ x 8½.
20468-5 Pa. $8.95

THE 100 GREATEST ADVERTISEMENTS, Julian Watkins. The priceless ingredient; His master's voice; 99 44/100% pure; over 100 others. How they were written, their impact, etc. Remarkable record. 130 illustrations. 233pp. 7⅞ x 10 3/5.
20540-1 Pa. $5.95

CRUICKSHANK PRINTS FOR HAND COLORING, George Cruickshank. 18 illustrations, one side of a page, on fine-quality paper suitable for watercolors. Caricatures of people in society (c. 1820) full of trenchant wit. Very large format. 32pp. 11 x 16.
23684-6 Pa. $5.00

THIRTY-TWO COLOR POSTCARDS OF TWENTIETH-CENTURY AMERICAN ART, Whitney Museum of American Art. Reproduced in full color in postcard form are 31 art works and one shot of the museum. Calder, Hopper, Rauschenberg, others. Detachable. 16pp. 8¼ x 11.
23629-3 Pa. $3.00

MUSIC OF THE SPHERES: THE MATERIAL UNIVERSE FROM ATOM TO QUASAR SIMPLY EXPLAINED, Guy Murchie. Planets, stars, geology, atoms, radiation, relativity, quantum theory, light, antimatter, similar topics. 319 figures. 664pp. 5⅜ x 8½.
21809-0, 21810-4 Pa., Two-vol. set $11.00

EINSTEIN'S THEORY OF RELATIVITY, Max Born. Finest semi-technical account; covers Einstein, Lorentz, Minkowski, and others, with much detail, much explanation of ideas and math not readily available elsewhere on this level. For student, non-specialist. 376pp. 5⅜ x 8½.
60769-0 Pa. $4.50

AMERICAN BIRD ENGRAVINGS, Alexander Wilson et al. All 76 plates. from Wilson's *American Ornithology* (1808-14), most important ornithological work before Audubon, plus 27 plates from the supplement (1825-33) by Charles Bonaparte. Over 250 birds portrayed. 8 plates also reproduced in full color. 111pp. 9⅜ x 12½. 23195-X Pa. $6.00

CRUICKSHANK'S PHOTOGRAPHS OF BIRDS OF AMERICA, Allan D. Cruickshank. Great ornithologist, photographer presents 177 closeups, groupings, panoramas, flightings, etc., of about 150 different birds. Expanded *Wings in the Wilderness*. Introduction by Helen G. Cruickshank. 191pp. 8¼ x 11. 23497-5 Pa. $6.00

AMERICAN WILDLIFE AND PLANTS, A. C. Martin, et al. Describes food habits of more than 1000 species of mammals, birds, fish. Special treatment of important food plants. Over 300 illustrations. 500pp. 5⅜ x 8½. 20793-5 Pa. $4.95

THE PEOPLE CALLED SHAKERS, Edward D. Andrews. Lifetime of research, definitive study of Shakers: origins, beliefs, practices, dances, social organization, furniture and crafts, impact on 19th-century USA, present heritage. Indispensable to student of American history, collector. 33 illustrations. 351pp. 5⅜ x 8½. 21081-2 Pa. $4.50

OLD NEW YORK IN EARLY PHOTOGRAPHS, Mary Black. New York City as it was in 1853-1901, through 196 wonderful photographs from N.-Y. Historical Society. Great Blizzard, Lincoln's funeral procession, great buildings. 228pp. 9 x 12. 22907-6 Pa. $8.95

MR. LINCOLN'S CAMERA MAN: MATHEW BRADY, Roy Meredith. Over 300 Brady photos reproduced directly from original negatives, photos. Jackson, Webster, Grant, Lee, Carnegie, Barnum; Lincoln; Battle Smoke, Death of Rebel Sniper, Atlanta Just After Capture. Lively commentary. 368pp. 8⅜ x 11¼. 23021-X Pa. $8.95

TRAVELS OF WILLIAM BARTRAM, William Bartram. From 1773-8, Bartram explored Northern Florida, Georgia, Carolinas, and reported on wild life, plants, Indians, early settlers. Basic account for period, entertaining reading. Edited by Mark Van Doren. 13 illustrations. 141pp. 5⅜ x 8½. 20013-2 Pa. $5.00

THE GENTLEMAN AND CABINET MAKER'S DIRECTOR, Thomas Chippendale. Full reprint, 1762 style book, most influential of all time; chairs, tables, sofas, mirrors, cabinets, etc. 200 plates, plus 24 photographs of surviving pieces. 249pp. 9⅞ x 12¾. 21601-2 Pa. $7.95

AMERICAN CARRIAGES, SLEIGHS, SULKIES AND CARTS, edited by Don H. Berkebile. 168 Victorian illustrations from catalogues, trade journals, fully captioned. Useful for artists. Author is Assoc. Curator, Div. of Transportation of Smithsonian Institution. 168pp. 8½ x 9½. 23328-6 Pa. $5.00

"OSCAR" OF THE WALDORF'S COOKBOOK, Oscar Tschirky. Famous American chef reveals 3455 recipes that made Waldorf great; cream of French, German, American cooking, in all categories. Full instructions, easy home use. 1896 edition. 907pp. 6⅝ x 9⅜.   20790-0 Clothbd. $15.00

COOKING WITH BEER, Carole Fahy. Beer has as superb an effect on food as wine, and at fraction of cost. Over 250 recipes for appetizers, soups, main dishes, desserts, breads, etc. Index. 144pp. 5⅜ x 8½. (Available in U.S. only)   23661-7 Pa. $2.50

STEWS AND RAGOUTS, Kay Shaw Nelson. This international cookbook offers wide range of 108 recipes perfect for everyday, special occasions, meals-in-themselves, main dishes. Economical, nutritious, easy-to-prepare: goulash, Irish stew, boeuf bourguignon, etc. Index. 134pp. 5⅜ x 8½.   23662-5 Pa. $2.50

DELICIOUS MAIN COURSE DISHES, Marian Tracy. Main courses are the most important part of any meal. These 200 nutritious, economical recipes from around the world make every meal a delight. "I . . . have found it so useful in my own household,"—N.Y. Times. Index. 219pp. 5⅜ x 8½.   23664-1 Pa. $3.00

FIVE ACRES AND INDEPENDENCE, Maurice G. Kains. Great back-to-the-land classic explains basics of self-sufficient farming: economics, plants, crops, animals, orchards, soils, land selection, host of other necessary things. Do not confuse with skimpy faddist literature; Kains was one of America's greatest agriculturalists. 95 illustrations. 397pp. 5⅜ x 8½.   20974-1 Pa. $3.95

A PRACTICAL GUIDE FOR THE BEGINNING FARMER, Herbert Jacobs. Basic, extremely useful first book for anyone thinking about moving to the country and starting a farm. Simpler than Kains, with greater emphasis on country living in general. 246pp. 5⅜ x 8½.   23675-7 Pa. $3.50

PAPERMAKING, Dard Hunter. Definitive book on the subject by the foremost authority in the field. Chapters dealing with every aspect of history of craft in every part of the world. Over 320 illustrations. 2nd, revised and enlarged (1947) edition. 672pp. 5⅜ x 8½.   23619-6 Pa. $7.95

THE ART DECO STYLE, edited by Theodore Menten. Furniture, jewelry, metalwork, ceramics, fabrics, lighting fixtures, interior decors, exteriors, graphics from pure French sources. Best sampling around. Over 400 photographs. 183pp. 8⅜ x 11¼.   22824-X Pa. $6.00

ACKERMANN'S COSTUME PLATES, Rudolph Ackermann. Selection of 96 plates from the Repository of Arts, best published source of costume for English fashion during the early 19th century. 12 plates also in color. Captions, glossary and introduction by editor Stella Blum. Total of 120pp. 8⅜ x 11¼.   23690-0 Pa. $4.50

SECOND PIATIGORSKY CUP, edited by Isaac Kashdan. One of the greatest tournament books ever produced in the English language. All 90 games of the 1966 tournament, annotated by players, most annotated by both players. Features Petrosian, Spassky, Fischer, Larsen, six others. 228pp. 5⅜ x 8½. 23572-6 Pa. $3.50

ENCYCLOPEDIA OF CARD TRICKS, revised and edited by Jean Hugard. How to perform over 600 card tricks, devised by the world's greatest magicians: impromptus, spelling tricks, key cards, using special packs, much, much more. Additional chapter on card technique. 66 illustrations. 402pp. 5⅜ x 8½. (Available in U.S. only) 21252-1 Pa. $4.95

MAGIC: STAGE ILLUSIONS, SPECIAL EFFECTS AND TRICK PHO-TOGRAPHY, Albert A. Hopkins, Henry R. Evans. One of the great classics; fullest, most authorative explanation of vanishing lady, levitations, scores of other great stage effects. Also small magic, automata, stunts. 446 illus-trations. 556pp. 5⅜ x 8½. 23344-8 Pa. $6.95

THE SECRETS OF HOUDINI, J. C. Cannell. Classic study of Houdini's incredible magic, exposing closely-kept professional secrets and revealing, in general terms, the whole art of stage magic. 67 illustrations. 279pp. 5⅜ x 8½. 22913-0 Pa. $4.00

HOFFMANN'S MODERN MAGIC, Professor Hoffmann. One of the best, and best-known, magicians' manuals of the past century. Hundreds of tricks from card tricks and simple sleight of hand to elaborate illusions involving construction of complicated machinery. 332 illustrations. 563pp. 5⅜ x 8½. 23623-4 Pa. $6.00

MADAME PRUNIER'S FISH COOKERY BOOK, Mme. S. B. Prunier. More than 1000 recipes from world famous Prunier's of Paris and London, specially adapted here for American kitchen. Grilled tournedos with anchovy butter, Lobster a la Bordelaise, Prunier's prized desserts, more. Glossary. 340pp. 5⅜ x 8½. (Available in U.S. only) 22679-4 Pa. $3.00

FRENCH COUNTRY COOKING FOR AMERICANS, Louis Diat. 500 easy-to-make, authentic provincial recipes compiled by former head chef at New York's Fitz-Carlton Hotel: onion soup, lamb stew, potato pie, more. 309pp. 5⅜ x 8½. 23665-X Pa. $3.95

SAUCES, FRENCH AND FAMOUS, Louis Diat. Complete book gives over 200 specific recipes: bechamel, Bordelaise, hollandaise, Cumberland, apri-cot, etc. Author was one of this century's finest chefs, originator of vichyssoise and many other dishes. Index. 156pp. 5⅜ x 8. 23663-3 Pa. $2.75

TOLL HOUSE TRIED AND TRUE RECIPES, Ruth Graves Wakefield. Authentic recipes from the famous Mass. restaurant: popovers, veal and ham loaf, Toll House baked beans, chocolate cake crumb pudding, much more. Many helpful hints. Nearly 700 recipes. Index. 376pp. 5⅜ x 8½. 23560-2 Pa. $4.50

HISTORY OF BACTERIOLOGY, William Bulloch. The only comprehensive history of bacteriology from the beginnings through the 19th century. Special emphasis is given to biography-Leeuwenhoek, etc. Brief accounts of 350 bacteriologists form a separate section. No clearer, fuller study, suitable to scientists and general readers, has yet been written. 52 illustrations. 448pp. 5⅝ x 8¼. 23761-3 Pa. $6.50

THE COMPLETE NONSENSE OF EDWARD LEAR, Edward Lear. All nonsense limericks, zany alphabets, Owl and Pussycat, songs, nonsense botany, etc., illustrated by Lear. Total of 321pp. 5⅜ x 8½. (Available in U.S. only) 20167-8 Pa. $3.95

INGENIOUS MATHEMATICAL PROBLEMS AND METHODS, Louis A. Graham. Sophisticated material from Graham *Dial*, applied and pure; stresses solution methods. Logic, number theory, networks, inversions, etc. 237pp. 5⅜ x 8½. 20545-2 Pa. $4.50

BEST MATHEMATICAL PUZZLES OF SAM LOYD, edited by Martin Gardner. Bizarre, original, whimsical puzzles by America's greatest puzzler. From fabulously rare *Cyclopedia*, including famous 14-15 puzzles, the Horse of a Different Color, 115 more. Elementary math. 150 illustrations. 167pp. 5⅜ x 8½. 20498-7 Pa. $2.75

THE BASIS OF COMBINATION IN CHESS, J. du Mont. Easy-to-follow, instructive book on elements of combination play, with chapters on each piece and every powerful combination team—two knights, bishop and knight, rook and bishop, etc. 250 diagrams. 218pp. 5⅜ x 8½. (Available in U.S. only) 23644-7 Pa. $3.50

MODERN CHESS STRATEGY, Ludek Pachman. The use of the queen, the active king, exchanges, pawn play, the center, weak squares, etc. Section on rook alone worth price of the book. Stress on the moderns. Often considered the most important book on strategy. 314pp. 5⅜ x 8½. 20290-9 Pa. $4.50

LASKER'S MANUAL OF CHESS, Dr. Emanuel Lasker. Great world champion offers very thorough coverage of all aspects of chess. Combinations, position play, openings, end game, aesthetics of chess, philosophy of struggle, much more. Filled with analyzed games. 390pp. 5⅜ x 8½. 20640-8 Pa. $5.00

500 MASTER GAMES OF CHESS, S. Tartakower, J. du Mont. Vast collection of great chess games from 1798-1938, with much material nowhere else readily available. Fully annotcd, arranged by opening for easier study. 664pp. 5⅜ x 8½. 23208-5 Pa. $7.50

A GUIDE TO CHESS ENDINGS, Dr. Max Euwe, David Hooper. One of the finest modern works on chess endings. Thorough analysis of the most frequently encountered endings by former world champion. 331 examples, each with diagram. 248pp. 5⅜ x 8½. 23332-4 Pa. $3.75

GEOMETRY, RELATIVITY AND THE FOURTH DIMENSION, Rudolf Rucker. Exposition of fourth dimension, means of visualization, concepts of relativity as Flatland characters continue adventures. Popular, easily followed yet accurate, profound. 141 illustrations. 133pp. 5⅜ x 8½.
23400-2 Pa. $2.75

THE ORIGIN OF LIFE, A. I. Oparin. Modern classic in biochemistry, the first rigorous examination of possible evolution of life from nitrocarbon compounds. Non-technical, easily followed. Total of 295pp. 5⅜ x 8½.
60213-3 Pa. $4.00

PLANETS, STARS AND GALAXIES, A. E. Fanning. Comprehensive introductory survey: the sun, solar system, stars, galaxies, universe, cosmology; quasars, radio stars, etc. 24pp. of photographs. 189pp. 5⅜ x 8½. (Available in U.S. only)
21680-2 Pa. $3.75

THE THIRTEEN BOOKS OF EUCLID'S ELEMENTS, translated with introduction and commentary by Sir Thomas L. Heath. Definitive edition. Textual and linguistic notes, mathematical analysis, 2500 years of critical commentary. Do not confuse with abridged school editions. Total of 1414pp. 5⅜ x 8½.
60088-2, 60089-0, 60090-4 Pa., Three-vol. set $18.50

Prices subject to change without notice.

Available at your book dealer or write for free catalogue to Dept. GI, Dover Publications, Inc., 180 Varick St., N.Y., N.Y. 10014. Dover publishes more than 175 books each year on science, elementary and advanced mathematics, biology, music, art, literary history, social sciences and other areas.